CRITICAL ACC[...]
SAND IN M[...]
EDITED BY JENNI[...]

D0720959

"A collection of ridiculous and sublime [...]
—*San Francisco Chronicle* Best-Seller List

"These snappy travel stories bursting with candor and crackling humor are sure to leave readers feeling that to not have an adventure to remember is a great loss indeed. *Sand in My Bra* will light a fire under the behinds of, as the dedication states, 'all the women who sit at home or behind their desks bitching that they never get to go anywhere.'"
—*Publishers Weekly*

"Reading about someone else's troubles can be devastatingly funny. And so we have in this volume exotic settings, language-based miscommunication, and not-always-pleasant surprises as things do not go as planned. Despite it all, our band of female travel writers laughs heartily, with pen, paper and laptop at the quick."
—*Chicago Tribune*

"The writers in *Sand in My Bra* revel in the absurdities of life away from home. F★★k epiphanies; these are the sort of yarns that leave me itching to hit the road."
—*BUST*

"Hip chicks with a flair for storytelling share travel tales in *Sand in My Bra*. From reveling in the "freedom to be fat" in Tahiti to cycling topless at the Burning Man festival in Nevada, the stories celebrate the unexpected joys of travel from a feminine perspective."
—*Orlando Sentinel*

"Good-natured women find the funny side of mishaps in places as far flung as the red-light district in Bangkok and a 50-pound sack race in small-town Nevada. There are plenty of laughs and—a side benefit—some handy warnings on what not to do when traveling."
—*Portsmith Herald*

"A delightfully entertaining look at atypical travel experiences."
—*South Coast Beacon*

"*Sand in My Bra* supplies laughs as well as a quick fix for the homebound yearning for a quick walk on the wild side."
—*St. Petersburg Times*

TRAVELERS' TALES BOOKS

Country and Regional Guides
America, Australia, Brazil, Central America, China, Cuba, France,
Greece, India, Ireland, Italy, Japan, Mexico, Nepal, Spain,
Thailand, Tibet, Turkey; American Southwest, Grand Canyon,
Hawai'i, Hong Kong, Paris, Provence, San Francisco, Tuscany

Women's Travel
Her Fork in the Road, A Woman's Europe, A Woman's Path,
A Woman's Passion for Travel, A Woman's World, Women in
the Wild, A Mother's World, Safety and Security for Women
Who Travel, Gutsy Women, Gutsy Mamas

Body & Soul
The Spiritual Gifts of Travel, The Road Within,
Love & Romance, Food, The Fearless Diner, The Adventure
of Food, The Ultimate Journey, Pilgrimage

Special Interest
Sand in My Bra and Other Misadventures, Not So Funny
When It Happened, The Gift of Rivers, Shitting Pretty,
Testosterone Planet, Danger!, The Fearless Shopper, The Penny
Pincher's Passport to Luxury Travel, The Gift of Birds,
Family Travel, A Dog's World, There's No Toilet Paper
on the Road Less Traveled, The Gift of Travel,
365 Travel, Adventures in Wine

Travel Literature
Coast to Coast, The Fire Never Dies, Kite Strings of the
Southern Cross, Last Trout in Venice, One Year Off, The Rivers
Ran East, The Royal Road to Romance, A Sense of Place,
Storm, The Sword of Heaven, Take Me With You, Trader Horn,
Unbeaten Tracks in Japan, The Way of the Wanderer

Whose panties are these ?

more misadventures from
funny women on the road

TRAVELERS' TALES

Whose panties are these ?

more misadventures from
funny women on the road

Edited by
JENNIFER L. LEO

Series Editors
JAMES O'REILLY AND LARRY HABEGGER

TRAVELERS' TALES
SAN FRANCISCO

Art Direction: Michele Wetherbee / Stefan Gutermuth
Interior design: Kathryn Heflin and Susan Bailey
Cover photograph: © Jim Baynes / Papau New Guinea Tours. Mudman of Papau
New Guinea.
Page layout: Patty Holden using the fonts Bembo and Journal

Distributed by: Publishers Group West, 1700 Fourth Street, Berkeley, California 94710.

Library of Congress Cataloging-in-Publication Data

Whose panties are these? : misadventures from funny women on the road / edited by Jennifer L. Leo — 1st ed.
    p. cm.
  ISBN 1-932361-11-1 (pbk.)
  1. Women travelers—Anecdotes. 2. Voyages and travels—Anecdotes.
3. Women travelers—Humor. 4. Voyages and travels—Humor. I. Leo, Jennifer L., 1971–

  G465 .W53 2004
  910.4'092'2—dc22

                                                            2004015603

First Edition
Printed in the United States
10 9 8 7 6 5 4 3 2 1

To the women who trade homes for vans, purses for backpacks,
boyfriends for plane tickets—and the mothers
who keep their worries to themselves.

Table of Contents

Introduction

Webster's defines *misadventure* as "a mishap; misfortune. " But doesn't that sound sterile? True misadventure is when someone who is taking herself too seriously gets schooled. Humbled. Sent to her room and told to "Think about it."

Because of the "adventure" half of the word, people associate misadventures with travel. And right they are. However, there is a big difference between misadventurists and whiners. The latter always *think* they are having misadventures. The former, well, they are the masters of the pub, the center of the circle, the great storytellers at the well. They know how to add the cheese to the whine and spin their story in such a way that we wind up snorting, crying, and doubling over begging for mercy instead of apologizing for their bum trip.

We've all seen (or been) the kind of tourist who bragged about her upcoming vacation or "business trip," fretted over packing and finding the best bump-me-up-to-first-class outfit, only to wind up on the flight from hell that lost her luggage. Folks, don't mistake this for the official prissy definition of misadventure—no, this is travel. The darker, smellier, rotten side of travel, but still travel just the same. You know why? Because it happens to everybody. And yes, your feet are supposed to hurt. If they didn't, you either didn't play hard enough or you're going home with the scoop on the best walking shoes on the market.

In both *Sand in My Bra* and *Whose Panties Are These?*
we've tried to go beyond the ordinary been-there-done-that
stories and bring you the outrageous. We've collected true
women's tales of trips that went south and have had the kind
of makeover to take them from groans to gutbusters. Why?
Because laughter is, and always will be, the best medicine.

The laughs in this book range from snappy one-liners to
pulling for heroines like Susan Lyn McCombs who saves her
friend from a preying Italian man in "Blind Faith," or Lynn
Santa Lucia who goes all out for a hunky fling in "Miami
Spice." Most of us can relate to a partner who pushes us over
the edge, but how many have the killer come-backs that
Felice Prager does in "Waiting for the Big 'O'" when her
new husband just doesn't get it? We would not want to
experience the beating that Bridget Kelso gets in "Open
Up and Say *Om*" on a visit to a spiritual healer in Nepal, or
share Liz Scott's horror at finding a burrowing bug in her
ear in "Entomology and Earplugs." But they sure make
good reading.

So, what's with the underwear titles? *Sand in My Bra*
represented the discomfort that trips gone awry can bring,
that icky, let-me-throw-aside-all-grace-and-dig-down-into-
my-bikini-top-to-get-the-itch-out feeling. But *Whose Panties
Are These?* I thought of this title because it reminded me of
my favorite joke that I played on someone else.

I was in Chicago for a book conference with Travelers'
Tales. We were staying at the Essex Hotel and were amused
by the burned out "Es" on their sign. To prolong the humor
I pulled out my sexiest purple lace string bikini and shoved
it in my pocket. When editor Sean O'Reilly and I walked
into his room, I slipped it into the sheets of his bed. He was
checking out the bathroom. When he uncovered the pair, he

started laughing. He just couldn't believe what he had found. Sniff check showed that both the undies and the sheets were clean.

It's been eight years. This will be the first time he finds out they were mine. Didn't think my butt was that small, eh, Sean? You'd be surprised what a girl will wear to look good at the right time.

—JENNIFER L. LEO

DEANNA SUKKAR

* * *

Underwear and Tear

What is ripening may not be the fruit.

I AWAKE AT THE CRACK OF DAWN TO INDIA'S NATIONAL
diversion, the Clearing of the Throat. Despite an official hotel
sign beseeching guests to refrain from such distasteful guttural
ablutions, as it "offends our Western visitors," the ritual
sounds push through the skinny walls. I swallow involuntarily.
In an effort to ignore the expectorate intrusion, I consider
my morning. A thought has been ruminating in my head for
several days. Foundations. No, not architectural marvels of
steel and glass, but underclothes, of weft and warp. A buying
urge is ripening. It is compellingly reinforced as I acknowl-
edge my frail underwear slung over the chair-post by my
backpack. After seven months of traveling, handwashing in
grotty sinks and freezing creeks, my cotton panties are puck-
ered, pulled, and pummeled, hardly recognizable, with innu-
merable gauzy portholes. I possess two more just like it. They
need to be laid to rest, granted neither a rag's reprieve, nor
reserved as emergency backup. I could put it off no longer. A
shopping jaunt to replace my porridge-colored panties is

clearly in order, a challenging task in the hot, congested, un-sophisticated streets of Bikaner.

After several fortifying cups of *chai*, I head to the bazaar with no small anticipation. Isn't this a land of silk saris and silver toe rings? Enough of my peripatetic, puritanical underclothes. I yearn to slip into something feminine, something new, something diaphanous. I cajole a girlfriend to come along and our movements are marked by all, including the cows. As foreigners and women in rural Rajasthan, it doesn't take long to acquire a curious entourage. Kiosks of corrugated metal line the dusty streets. Officious shopkeepers, invariably men, clutch smoldering *bidis* and breathe smooth words as I approach. "Looking is free, madam!" "A Punjabi suit for you?" "What is your price, madam?" One slight hesitation, one backward glance, a catch of the eye, a few steps slower than normal...any of these and one is caught by a shrewd salesman, the spark of the hunt in his eye.

Within several minutes, like an amateur, I slip up. I am sucked into the sales vortex, immediately surrounded by men in colorful turbans wrapped like taffy, brilliant yellows, oranges, and reds. Inquisitive kohl-eyed children jostle to gain vantage. A number of old men gather, darkened with age, sun, and dirt. Women, their bangles tinkling, peek out from behind colorful veils, then tuck back in like bashful turtles. This brazen scrutiny is not an unusual occurrence in India, but it is the first time I am underwear shopping, and incontestably, the first time I have to do so in an open air market. No, this is not going to be an easy purchase.

So many boxes. So many hands. Quickly, covers are tossed off with the speed and precision of a tumbling formation of dominoes. Their contents spill out onto the counter. Dozens of hopeful panties await my inspection. No less than five zealous men, in fitted white shirts, are falling over themselves and their boxes to help me. Let the games begin!

Indian women are petite. The largest panty presented, is an embarrassingly diminutive affair. Impossible. Hands pressed together in front of him, the avuncular proprietor states with conviction, "No, madam, good fit!" A sea of heads nod in accord. For the briefest of moments, I almost succumb. Not only would the act swiftly bring a close to this public ordeal, but I am flattered that they think I could fit into underwear the size of a tea cozy. I hear a snicker from my friend, who probably *could* fit into them. I sigh at the missed opportunity to abandon ship and emphatically shake my head. It is becoming apparent that I am one demanding customer who would require advanced handling and encouragement.

From more corners are brought more boxes. Lids are flying and knickers are piling. Lace-free, waist-high, the color selection is severely limited: cardamom green, tusk white, ginger beige. The counter resembles the Himalayas. The owner is dispatching designated runners to the adjoining stalls to lug back, pardon the pun, more booty. We are progressing. Underwear that I could fit into when I was twelve. I smile. Twenty more years to go. Clearly an active visual is needed. I grab one particularly natty number, hook my thumb in the waistband and anchor it to my left side. All eyes are glued to my hips. Unhurriedly, I proceed to pull the elastic to its limit. Three-quarters across my childbearing girth and it would stretch no further. The audience goes wild with comprehension. "Ahhhhh!!!"

Several demonstrations later (O.K., I *am* milking the crowd, but they are so damn easy), we are circling a prey of size eighty. Clueless as to their sizing system, nevertheless optimistic, I give each one the tug-of-war test. Close, so close. The crowd titters with possibility. "Perhaps…" says one unctuous man. We all wait. A pregnant pause made more so when he notices me indecorously staring at the two gold dots embedded in his two front teeth. They remind me of a pair of dice, rolled snake eyes. He ripples and preens with import, but doesn't miss a transactional beat. Diplomatically, he continues, "Perhaps…a 100 would suit?" On cue, the five angular clerks turn like Venetian blinds and again begin rummaging in the diminishing stacked boxes. Nice. We've hit three digits.

Proudly, a *chapati*-thin salesman spins around with what I can only describe as a battle cry of victory. A mushroom-colored velour panty. All eyes light up expectantly. This is a crowd pleaser. I am thinking, velour? Are you nuts? Was it made from leftover coffin lining? It's an inch thick. I could use it for insulation. "Um, no, uh, thanks." Crestfallen and defeated, the vendor deflates. We have our first fatality. We are down to four tenacious peddlers.

The next up, with a veteran's calm, quiets everyone. He cradles what he trusts will be a sure winner. The cutting edge in bottom wear. Necks are craning. Why it's…it's… it's a pair of men's briefs?!? I quickly, *graciously*, point out this disparity. So keen to please, everyone has already slipped into a con-gratulatory mode at the imminent purchase. "But these are for MEN!" I cry desperately. Ineffective. Really, I have no choice. Demo! Demo! Gather round. I push all panties aside, no small feat, and put the renegade shorts on the counter, spreading them out as flat as men's briefs can be flattened. I then stick my closed fist in the pouch reserved for, well, what I do not have, and brilliantly, loudly, triumphantly, re-declare, "These are men's shorts!" Exhibiting admirable restraint, I refrain from poking my fingers through the aperture. Giggles erupt from the grown men; palms fly up to the mouths of the women. Their eyes dance.

About this time, I decide that my three utilitarian panties, beloved and loyal, are surely good for another month. Why not buy the fetching velour pair and satisfy the now rabid masses? What's more, they would make for a great story-slash-great pillow-slash-adequate sink plug. Besides, lunchtime is looming and the thought of hot *poori* is edging out underwear. I am hungry. My hand dips into my pocket for rupees.

Unexpectedly, from the bowels of the store, one of the five (well, four) finds a box and lifts it above our heads. If it were gilded and set with rubies, a gift from Holy Ganesh, it could not have been met with more prospect. The carton is stamped "105." The young salesman is beaming. His associates are beaming. I am beaming. Bikaner is beaming. Like a progeny of Pandora, I lift the lid, silently whispering, yea, chanting, the Beatles lyric, *Let it be! Let it be*! After a cursory glance, not wanting to squander the energy of the crowd, I joyfully, almost tearfully, lift out of the box a banana-colored panty with an intriguingly stretchy disposition. Like a trophy, like a babe, I raise it high for all to see. I am awash in an angelic mantle of brilliant white teeth and brown eyes gazing upward. The man is a hero and I can return to relative anonymity.

Up until now, my silently amused friend, who has neither left my side nor come to my aid, finally feels the need to utter one word, a word that throws our exhilarated sales clerks into panic. "Sexy!" she quips in her high-pitched Australian accent. The action behind the counter comes to a dead stop. Exhausted and chagrined, apprehensive looks are exchanged. The eldest salesman recovers first. Evidently fearing that my virtue has been brought into question, he unobtrusively, confidently, leans across the counter, "Oh, no. Nooooo, madam," he reassuringly whispers, "these are *not* sexy!"

Deanna Sukkar is a professional chef currently exploring avenues of self-expression that do not involve sauces or sugar. She has eaten her way across most of the continents but finds she is still hungry. At the moment, she is neither wielding her chef's knife, nor looking for global flavors, but is homebound in Seattle obtaining a Master's Degree in Library and Information Science. Her craving for travel remains unsated.

*

The elixir is poured into an empty bottle. Ngoh-Fonseka translates, "Make your husband's coffee using this water. He will have eyes only for you. And now she will bless the rest of the water for a potion to splash on your face. You must do it every day. When either potion depletes, you can top it up with normal water. It will not lose its potency." Ngoh-Fonseka smiles. "She wants to know if you want to know a persuasive potion you can make at home?"

In a culture where it is still permissible for a man to have four wives and where women's rights aren't exactly at the forefront of political discussion, it is perfectly logical that such secrets and potions exist. This kind of covert knowledge gives a woman power in her situation, not unlike our North American equivalent of wearing Victoria's Secret red-hot lingerie under our beige clothes.

"Bring it on," I say.

There is a rapid Malaysian discussion. There are smiles and gestures. Finally, I can't stand it any longer. "What? What do I do at home?" Ngoh-Fonseka brings her hand to her mouth, smiling, "Boil your panties and use the water to make your husband a hot drink."

—Colleen Friesen, "Love Potion No. 9"

* ✱ *

The Chicken Theory

I'll have what she's having.

"ALI, HOW COME ALL LEBANESE GIRLS HAVE BIG BREASTS?" I whispered across the breakfast table. "Is it silicone?"

It was ten o'clock on a Monday morning in a trendy restaurant of central Beirut. Ali followed my gaze and glanced at the group of young women settling in at the table next to us. All wore low-cut stretch tops that could barely hold their disproportionately large bosoms.

Turning his big black eyes back to me, Ali just clicked his tongue and jerked his chin up at me in that off-putting Arab way of saying no. Then, between two sips of mint tea, he solemnly declared:

"Too much chicken."

"Chicken?"

"Eah."

"What chicken? You mean chicken as in *dijaaj*?"

"Eah."

"Ya Ali, just what the hell are you talking about?"

Ali explained that, for the last few years, Lebanon's farmers had been feeding shameless amounts of hormones to their chicken to fatten them faster, practically cutting in half the time required for a chick to reach maturity. Lebanese, and for this I can testify, eat tremendous amounts of chicken. Unfortunately—or fortunately—the local stock was now so full of hormones that, according to Ali's theory, it had altered the female population's body proportions.

"When you go to the Middle East, remember that everything you know is wrong," an Arab friend of mine had advised before I left my Montreal home. With this in mind, I gave Ali a fake smile and stared into my cup of tea, working hard on opening my foreign mind to the notion that a steady diet of chicken made Lebanese women grow enormous breasts. As far as I was concerned, I had been eating chicken *shawarma* sandwiches for breakfast, lunch, and dinner for a week by then and it looked to me like my pants were filling up much faster than my bra!

That very afternoon, however, empirical evidence from what I considered a significantly more reliable source was provided to me to back up Ali's claim. I got stranded in the Chouf Mountains and hitched a ride with a friendly local who insisted I visit his German wife. She would, he claimed, be most delighted to entertain foreign company. I had no set plans so I spent the afternoon in a fabulous mountaintop villa with the elegant and well-traveled Karine talking about religion, politics, and…chicken.

"You know, it's not as crazy as it sounds," sensible Karine said of Ali's theory. "I would actually believe chicken could be what's behind it," she added, leaving me choking on my peppermint tea.

"I'm serious!" she insisted. "I used to feed my female German shepherd scraps of chicken and I had to stop because the hormones were affecting her period."

I left Karine's villa that day with as many doubts in my mind as there were tea stains on my shirt. Could it really be the chicken?

Hopelessly intrigued, I traveled all over the land of the great cedar trees shaking my incredulous head at the multitude of slender—yet extraordinarily shapely—Lebanese girls I encountered. From Tripoli to Tyre, throughout Beirut, Byblos, Sidon, Bcharré, and Baalbek, those chicken hormones seemed to have spared no one with an XX chromosome.

And what about the guys? I couldn't help but wonder. What could be the most likely effect of growth hormones on the male anatomy? Encouraged by my own speculations, I spent endless afternoons hiding in restaurant corners, riding crowded buses, or walking aimlessly along the corniche to spy on Lebanese men and steal inquisitive glances at their

—————)—————

I t's the old chicken-and-egg question: Are people fat because they come to Las Vegas, or do they come to Vegas because they're fat? To find the answer, I approached the Vegas altar, the buffet, and I "splurged" an unlucky $13 on the stylish luncheon at the Bellagio. Its supermarket of dishes could easily give an eater an anxiety attack and put her in a diabetic coma. Bowls of mixed chocolates and baskets of focaccia, cow and pig killed and cured two dozen ways, seven varieties of seafood salad, five kinds of pickles, and everything else edible short of a partridge in a pear tree. It was clear that people were fat here because they ate too much chicken *and* eggs.

♦

—April Thompson,
"Lost in Las Vegas"

crotches. Could this little land breed men of larger-than-life manliness?

Alas, unable to verify so enticing a hypothesis, I gave in to my skepticism and discarded the chicken theory as pure fancy. Chicken? Oh, please! What a far-fetched idea.

Yet reason seldom defeats wishful thinking. I still ate chicken *shawarma* three times a day, continued—in vain—to monitor my bra's fit every morning, and smiled at Lebanese men a lot.

I did not speak of chicken again until the night before I left Lebanon. I was just about to fall asleep in my hard little Beirut bed when Rachelle, my Aussie dorm mate, broke our late night silence:

"Is it me or do Lebanese girls all have big boobs?"

I grinned like a Cheshire cat in the darkness.

"Too much chicken."

"Chicken?"

"Eah."

Christine Michaud has lived, worked, and traveled extensively throughout the Middle East. Her stories have appeared in Sand in My Bra and Other Misadventures, *BootsnAll.com, Worldhum.com, and Vagabonding.net. She lives in Montreal.*

* ✴ *

Cabin Pressure

There's nothing quite like a little time in the country.

ESCAPE—YOU MIGHT THINK IT'S WHAT YOU DESIRE. UNTIL you've actually run somewhere. Then, sometimes you realize all you want is to be back in the terrible cracked talons of your captors.

Take a few weekends ago, when my man Marty suddenly turned to me and piped, "Hey, let's go stay at a cabin in the woods! We need a break, some time away. We've been working like *dawgs!*"

This was striking for several reasons. 1) *I'm* the one with the frequent, powerful B&B-and-cabin fantasies, and 2) he's the one who wants to stay home and follow the NFC. These are our roles. Our destiny. But hell, I wasn't going to look a gift horse in the butt.

"Hallelujah" I testified. Marty got on the Internet, and quickly found an ideal destination: a cozy cabin nestled on eighty snow-covered acres in West Virginia. The web site indicated the place was owned by two aging hippies who provide all guests with granola and soy milk. "Count me *in*," I said.

Marty rang them up and luck was on our side: it seemed that, just a few short weeks before the Martin Luther King holiday weekend—when everything else was booked—a cabin remained magically available. Marty booked it and I sighed, visions of healthy breakfasts, scorched kindling, and nature walks dancing in my head.

Flash forward two weeks: Winding past old country churches and farms, we pulled onto what would have been a dirt road if there hadn't been so much snow, and there he was: Dave, one of the aged hippies. Simultaneously rickety yet robust, Dave brought to mind the praying mantis. He was jovial, formerly blond but now mostly gray with big blue eyes. He seemed excited to meet us. I looked down. Dave's khaki pants had clearly been worn several days in a row without laundering, because, well, maybe that's how it's done in the country.

Next, things got tense as our silly, sorry city car fishtailed all over the place while we followed Dave's truck deep into the woods, finally stopping at a beckoning little brown cabin set on a slope. We scrambled to the door, hungry to behold the interior of our home for the next three days. And there it was, finally stretching out before us: a rustic, simple one-room abode outfitted stem to stern in thrift-store finds. My eyes fell over the nubby plaid couch, the ceramic black panther skulking across a dresser, the macramé-owl wall-hanging the size of a mini-dress. I dug them.

And I dug that there were no vestiges of modern life here—no phone, no TV, and, most notably, no connection to a sewer system. It only took a few seconds to realize being in the country meant that a loud *click-suck, click-suck* noise would emanate from an in-house water pump whenever one copped a squat or washed a beer mug. Yeah, we were truly in the middle of nowhere, tethered to nothing. Just me, Marty, and a milk carton cut in half and left behind by Dave in the hopes that we'd compost.

After a few hours of fireside reading, restlessness set in and we were compelled to explore the snowy acreage at our disposal. We suited up like nobody's business—me shielding the lion's share of my face with a balaclava I ordered from a harsh-weather-gear catalog as a joke when I lived in Louisiana—and headed out to follow Dave's hand-drawn map. As we trudged, we had some giggles trying to identify the mysterious animal tracks in the snow. Were they from deer? Wildebeest? Wayward salmon? Hell, we didn't know.

Within about six minutes, it became apparent: all trails led to Dave and his wife's renovated Civil War-era home. *Gosh, did they want company that bad? Or were they narcissists? And hey, where was his wife, anyway?* We went ahead and loitered in their backyard for a spell feeling awkward and admiring the cheerful outhouse and sizeable man-made pond—afraid to proceed on the trail, which led to the front of the house.

Not knowing what else to do, Marty and I turned back. But then suddenly, like a daddy long legs appearing out of nowhere on your corn dog, there he was, the spindly Dave, just standing there at the other end of the pond staring in our direction, silent. Reflexively, I called out to him. Dave gave a friendly holler and a wave, and we all commenced to moving along the trail toward each other. Meeting at the edge of the frozen pond, the three of us passed the next eight minutes, hands in pockets, chatting about city life vs. country life vs. suburban hell. I kept thinking Dave's wife would emerge from the house (or the outhouse) and join in, but she never did. Last, we kvetched about how it was supposed to dip to four degrees that night, then we went our separate ways. Dave seemed to be a good guy. We didn't want to think weird thoughts about him, but we couldn't help it.

"Is Dave going to kill us?" I asked Marty on the way back to the cabin.

"Probably not," he said. "But I can't promise anything."

After spaghetti in the cabin, Marty left for a night hike by the light of the full moon so he could experience four degrees. I was having nothing to do with that; for me, the time had come for the cornerstone of any relaxing weekend: a hot bath accompanied by wine and a book. With a self-satisfied grin, I bid Marty good-bye and began to fill the tub. But alas, the smile dropped abruptly when I walked in the bathroom five minutes later and saw that the recycled well water spewing from the tap looked like someone had not only peed in the tub, but crapped in it as well. My stomach lurched to the left. But then denial snapped firmly into place. I *had to* get in this bath. I *would* get into this bath, even if it spelled dysentery. I poured in lots of bubble bath then, steeled myself and slid into the bilge. And, it wasn't that bad—the poo juice. If it touched your lips, it made them numb, I discovered—but that was O.K. What wasn't O.K. was the temperature. The water, it turned out, was about as warm as a mug of A&W root beer. I downed my wine like it was a shot. That helped quiet the involuntary gasping.

A few hours later, with the cabin aglow from the fire, Marty and I dropped off into a Zenned-out sleep, expecting our next waking thoughts to arrive about ten hours later, containing sentiments such as: "Ahhh, the healing properties of the wilderness!" Instead, those thoughts came in just three hours, and included phrases like: "What?" and "Oh, *shit.*"

At 2:30 A.M., my eyes flew open in alarm and my pulse spiked from coma level to jogging pace. It wasn't anything I saw; it was what I heard: *click-suck, click-suck, click-suck*—the sound the water pump made when someone in the cabin was using water. I felt around in the bed—was Marty up taking a leak? I found his arm, warm, filled with the paralysis of sleep. He was right there.

O.K., so then *who* was using water? Who had activated the *click-suck*?

My heart lodged itself in my throat. Really, there were only two possible explanations: either it was a ghost come to taunt us, or there were murderous hooligans spraying a hose on the outside of the cabin as a mean-spirited prelude our violent murders, which would likely happen in the next thirty to forty-five minutes.

"Hear that?! Hear that?!" I scream-whispered to Marty, waking him up then regaling him with my theories. Marty was not acceptably panicked.

"Relax," he said wearily. "I'll get the flashlight and check it out. And I'll look out the windows. But I bet it's the cabin's water system trying to suck water from the well, and maybe it can't because of the weather."

"Or maybe it's Jack from *The Shining*," I trilled, not kidding, envisioning Dave skulking around near the back deck. As Marty crossed the cabin in the dark with only the eerie, amber beam of the flashlight lighting the way, I stayed in bed with the musty comforter pulled up to my clavicle. I tracked him carefully, expecting at any minute to see an ax come out of nowhere and slice his torso cleanly in half. When that didn't happen, I took to passing the excruciating minutes peering out the skylights in the cabin's vaulted ceiling. Through them, I saw only innocent objects like the dusty-purple sky, the luminous moon, and the tops of the pines. But I assumed it was only seconds before some manifestation of the Mothman revealed itself, flapping its wings and hovering out there peering in. We were, after all, in West Virginia.

No matter how much Marty stared at the pump, the unexplained *click-sucking* kept on unabated. I flashed back to the scene earlier in the evening, one that now seemed rife with wanton disregard for safety and common sense: Marty out walking alone in the snow and me in the cabin alone, *in the bathtub.* My god, were we trying to create the perfect horror movie scene? Were we *trying* to invite Jason?

Marty returned to the bed, unable to remedy the matter or see anything of note.

"I also checked for monsters," he said.

> ———— ☽ ————
>
> **O**h yeah, I have memories of West Virginia. Two. One was cycling past a teenager with a shotgun in the doorway of his trailer. The other was being chased by three dogs while riding on a Rails to Trails path. That taught me to stay with the group.
>
> ◆
>
> —Jennifer L. Leo, "'You're Exotic' and Other Cute Things the Locals Said"

"Shut up," I snarled.

Just then, we heard a sound like twigs breaking outside. I lay there gritting my teeth and feeling so sorry that we'd not heretofore become members of the NRA, or at least the North American Pepper Spray Club. We were sitting ducks out there, stooges. My god, it was terrible in the country. *Why do people do it?* I wondered. *Why do they come to isolated places where bad things happen—terrible, evil things—and you can't call the cops and even if you could, it'd take at least four days for them to respond?* I couldn't sort it all out in my head. I just hoped against hope we'd still be there in the morning to say to Dave: What the hell?

Nothing came of the twig noises, but the *click-sucking* was unceasing. Reclining there stiff as a coffin lid and amped to the gills on adrenaline, my central nervous system spinning wildly on its axis, the metered noise was starting to sound an awful lot like an old ghost woman pressing down time and time again on the peddles of an ancient, broken sewing machine. *Click-suck, click-suck. Click-suck.* She was tired, but persistent—would keep at it through eternity. She had to get those socks darned, those pantaloons mended. But she couldn't, not with us mortals there scarfing spaghetti, taking poo baths, and invading her space.

I wanted to get up and get my little book light from the kitchen table so I could try to read in order to calm myself down. But I was too scared to leave the bed, too scared to even let an arm or leg dangle over the edge of the mattress, because of, you know, creatures, entities. I tried to think of an indirect way of making Marty go get the light, but I couldn't.

Suddenly, an inner voice showed up to berate me. *Christ in a sidecar, what's your problem? Twenty-five years ago, you were the little girl who would open up the front door and walk outside at night if you heard weird noises, ready to kickbox intruders. And you walk through the valley of the shadow of death in your neighborhood all the time and you don't flinch, and now, out here, you're scared of ghosts? What gives?*

The voice had a point. But I had no idea what gave.

Then I remembered that just a week prior, my sister had put me on the phone with my six-year-old niece, who'd just awakened petrified that something mysterious was going to maul her in the night. *I* had talked her down from her little-girl ledge.

"Brooke, listen, there are no monsters."

"How do you *know*?" she'd pined.

"I know. I *really do* know. I promise you, tomorrow you will want to call me and say, 'Gosh, you were right—no monsters *or* bad people caused any problems in the night.'"

And Brooke bought it. Now, why couldn't I?

Then suddenly—sweet Vishnu!—an hour after the sound had begun, it stopped, replacing itself with a roaring silence. For me, post-traumatic stress disorder kicked right in and I had to stay up listening for possible tortured specters fluttering by or young toughs skittering outside. This, while Marty, satisfied all was well, passed right out. After about an hour of torturous hand-wringing, then sweats followed by chills, most of my cacophonous bad imagery faded. Miraculously, at about 5 A.M., so did I.

When we finally woke up, neither bloodied nor dismembered, Marty and I marched right over to Dave's, emboldened by the daylight. At first, Dave stood on his porch pinching at his scruffy hair growth and looking bewildered by our story, which I felt confirmed my sewing-lady theory. As he took time to cogitate, I subtly backed up a few steps to look in his upstairs windows, angling to catch a glimpse of what I thought might be his wife, long dead and propped up in a rocking chair, just like the mom in the movie *Psycho*. But the windows were reflective and I couldn't see anything like that in there.

"Oh! Whoops," Dave suddenly erupted. "I must have set the water filtration system to go off in the middle of the night. Oh, I'm *so sorry!*" Then he said all we had to do to sidestep the horror the following night was flip two fuse switches near the bathroom.

Most of me believed the man, but the remaining 22 percent remained skeptical. I had to wonder: If his hippie filtration apparatus was set to go off in the wee hours, loud as bones rattling, hadn't guests complained before? Or, had the triple homicide that I suspect took place in that cabin a few years back kept all guests away? Because, come on, why else would the place be available so close to a holiday weekend?

For the rest of the trip then, with my fight-or-flight mechanism idling in first gear, everything took on an evil tenor. The tracks we spotted in the snow by our door—apparently from deer—seemed to me to have come from the cloven-hooved one. The tiny single red light visible under our cabin—which was probably a light attached to a generator or something—seemed like a devil eye recording all our comings and goings. Everywhere, I saw little Blair Witch twig sculptures in the trees. Inside the cabin, I started to feel that the macramé owl/mini-dress was staring at me, mocking me, as was the old restored photograph of an Indian chief looking pensive with a stuffed quail on his head. And at any minute, I was certain we'd see Dave standing by our car staring blankly but purposefully at the cabin.

That night, our last night there, Marty tried to tune in a game on the outdated radio and what came through instead was our wedding song, Dido's "Thank You." He stood, holding out his hand. I stood, too, accepting the invitation, and we danced in front of a big bay window that had no curtains— a big giant window, beyond which stretched nothing but woods and snow and the black of night. *This is it,* I thought, *the moment the sniper has been waiting for.* But soon the song ended. Our lives didn't. *Whew.*

And Dave, it seemed, was correct: flipping those switches did do the trick. That night we slept ten hours with nary a visitation, and then high-tailed it out of there in the morning. Back to my city where the sirens sometimes drown out my phone calls and the building manager periodically puts up signs in the elevator that read, "Look out. Someone was robbed at knifepoint one street over," where the young toughs are cocky enough to break into cars at three in the afternoon, and where shootouts happen outside the corner grocery.

Ah, my lovely, lovely city where cops are abundant and people can hear you scream.

Sired in South Florida and seasoned in New Orleans, Suz Redfearn now meanders mostly around Falls Church, Virginia. When she's not yanking humping dogs off her Golden Retriever puppy at the dog park, Redfearn pens essays and articles for Salon, The Washington Post, Men's Health, Fit Pregnancy *and* Health *magazine. She's currently toiling away on a memoir about her mess of a destination wedding, which, it just so happened, was 1) scheduled to begin the day after Sept. 11, and 2) located right in the path of Hurricane Gabrielle.*

WENDY SOREF

* * *

Where the Size of Your Butt Matters

Booty is in the eye of the beholder.

I HAVE A SMALL BUTT. IT IS ROUND AND, ALTHOUGH IT JUTS out a little bit, it is by no means a focal point. It fits into the pants of my generation just fine, which is probably why I never gave it a second thought. When a body-conscious friend would ask me if her butt looked fat in a particular pair of black pants, I would grimace, "It looks fine." As a friend, I tried to be patient and understanding, but in fat-butt insecurity situations I could never muster much sympathy. That is, until I myself began to teeter on tiptoes, peering around at my rear in a grimy mirror in a bathroom in Senegal, asking myself, "Does my butt look scrawny?"

My time as a study-abroad student in Senegal was marked by many revelations. One of them was this: For the first time in my life, my butt was hopelessly inadequate. It did not swagger or jiggle or swing as I walked through the neighborhood. My pants did not cling seductively to the curves of my caboose. My cheeks did not pillow into a heart beneath me as I sat down because, sadly, they had nowhere to go.

The Senegalese women I knew generally did not have this problem. Their curves tucked at the hips and then expanded gently like cushions beneath them to absorb the shocks produced by the potholes and cracks tripped over by the wobbly mini-buses we rode to get around town. My female friends leisurely sauntered around the *quartier* so that each hip cocked out one at a time and in the release, bounced back just so. Men nearby, from the businessman in the sleekest tailored suit checking his watch to the older gentleman in a knit cap slumped on a bench by the curb, perked to attention as my friends would slowly glide by. In Senegal, the female posterior is an object of reverence and it did not take long for me to realize that there was very little of my backside to revere.

Nor did my gluteus inadequacy escape the attention of my Senegalese host family. The mealtime chant, *"Il faut manger! Lekkal!* It is necessary to eat! Eat!"* was a standard tune around our communal bowl. My host sister, Kiné, ensured that the metallic bottom of my triangular portion of the bowl was never exposed by pushing rice out from the center and piling more vegetables and fish in front of me. Sure, these daily interactions were motivated by the Senegalese tradition of heaping hospitality, but this did not stand alone. My family explicitly informed me that they planned to send back an improved, more attractive Wendy to the States, a softer Wendy, a more substantial Wendy, a Wendy with a big butt.

My American friends who were more generously endowed in the booty department were subject to a different kind of scrutiny. They endured daily catcalls of lustful admiration from both strangers and friends. Exasperated, self-conscious, and vulnerable, they would respond, "You just can't tell an American girl that she has a big butt, even if it is a compliment!" "Well, you are not in America anymore," the back-side enthusiasts would reply. This being a pretty good point, I began to observe changes in my friends' behavior. My once-insecure friends returned from the market with the spandex-like jeans that were the rage among our Senegalese female peers and wore them to the red-plush-mirrored, TV-movie-esque nightclubs of Dakar, to shake and grind defiantly on the dance floor. Where earlier in the year, an unidentified man hissing about the size of a friend's derrière would cause her to drop her shoulders and head and to tighten her mouth, in time, she might be inspired to thrust her shoulders back, fix her eyes ahead, and even smile.

As a group of enlightened American women we were sure we would never concede to this brand of what many would consider objectification, and we certainly never expected to revel in it. Yet, as the Senegalese tell it, catcalls are not merely the vessels of lust or oppression, but an opening for appreciation of the luscious mystery of the female form. Although my backside was rarely in the streetside spotlight, my general appearance stirred many a hiss and holler as I walked to the university, the bakery, or the bus stop. When I complained to my Senegalese host sister, Boundaw, how I hated all the attention, she looked at me with a smirk, "Oh, I like it very much. I'll take yours." In my first vulnerable, doubt-wracked months, I would have gladly handed Boundaw all the anony-mous compliments the exotic appeal of my white skin and blond hair garnered; yet, somehow what initially felt like a daily assault became a daily affirmation. In fact, when I received fewer sidewalk accolades, I wondered, "What? I don't look cute today?" At least, that's how I felt on the pow-erful days. The golden-tressed lioness days. The days when I could talk to anyone, shake their hand, and canoodle their baby. But there were other days when the stifling heat and poverty choked my fearlessness, when I didn't want to see the young mother with pink scars on her ankles and a newborn in her arms, parked in the dirt, begging for food or spare change, and I didn't want her, or anyone else, to see me.

In Senegal, women are often marginalized in the general economy, but they are fierce participants in the rickety street-side one. Almost every household offers a mother or a daughter to the curb to sell mango slices, toothbrush twigs, bags of sugared peanuts, frozen bissap juices in plastic baggies, and *fonde*—sugary balls of doughy goo. *Jaay fonde amul pertiman*. Or "Sell *fonde*, have no loss." This is the first line of a song about *fonde* and sexual politics. It is sung in every courtyard, market, and high school, essentially wherever women congregate to gossip and tease and cook. The song instructs: don't worry if you don't sell your *fonde*, it is really better if you eat it yourself, because it will fatten up your behind. The underlying message of this anthem is that a chunky bottom will catch the attention of a handsome beau or sustain the interest of a husband who is easily distracted and who may well bring another woman into your house as his second wife, the recurrent nightmare of wives trapped in Senegal's polygamous tangle. In this way, "*jaay fonde*" has entered the popular lexicon to mean a chubby rear and to be

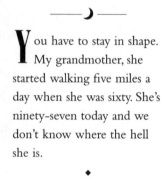

You have to stay in shape. My grandmother, she started walking five miles a day when she was sixty. She's ninety-seven today and we don't know where the hell she is.

♦

—Ellen Degeneres

"*jaay fonde*" is to be healthy, feminine, and sensual. Beyond sexual desire, "*jaay fonde*" is an imperative; your Senegalese mother will tell you so.

In a Senegalese marriage, there are several interconnected assumptions: the husband will provide for the family, the wife will bear many children, and said wife will balloon to twice her previous size. A large wife is the unambiguous symbol of a family's prosperity and an indication of a husband's ability to bring home the mutton. The Senegalese dietary staples of starchy white rice, baguettes, and fatty vegetable oil sold by the gallon contribute to this triangular prophecy. I met a Canadian nutrition student who studied diabetes and anemia among women in a community outside Dakar. Many of the women she spoke with were ultimately unwilling to risk losing weight by using oil sparingly and cooking with hearty, healthy Senegalese couscous instead of rice. Somehow, a healthier lifestyle was not worth the risk of shedding social status and straining marital satisfaction.

If sexual norms are created, not out of desire or arbitrary preferences, but out of functional necessity, then in Senegal, wide childbearing hips have been selected generation after generation to pop out babies to fill the fields of millet, maize, and then sugar cane and rice, and then cotton and peanuts. As the Sahara Desert has crept with sinister silence into Senegal, as droughts have struck tired soil and villagers, agrarian life has been weakened. Young men and women flood the cities, hopeful that industrialization will hit before famine does. In the city, where material expectations swell, modern mothers and fathers with gainful employment have begun to choose a car, a cell phone, or a television set over more mouths to feed. A digital and glossy assault of skinny women has already been launched from Occidental headquarters.

Could "*jaay fonde*" go out of vogue as the anticipated wave of modernization selects butts like mine? Perhaps, when Dakar freezes over. Besides the fact that most Senegalese laborers are still engaged in a farm economy, my imagination cannot begin to stretch around a Senegal without "*jaay fonde.*" Returning from Senegal, I saw new beauty in my friends' behinds and the wide hips of my mother's pear-shaped frame. I know that I shall never look at any butt the same way again, and if my new aesthetic preference can defend itself against the circus of shrinking American women, I do believe "*jaay fonde*" will endure among those nursed from the start on its mysterious succulence.

After six months or so in Dakar, every time I turned my back, I began to rouse chuckles and comments from my host mother about my ballooning butt. Soon, my tailor remarked with a raised eyebrow that my hips were a couple of centimeters wider than before, to the amusement of everyone in the shop. Next, my sister pinched my rear and exclaimed, "*Oooh, am nga jaay fonde leggi!* You are *jaay fonde* now!" Despite the reinforcement of a chorus of similar comments, I have to be honest with myself: my butt never actually grew; these remarks were really just subtle affirmations of acceptance and affection. Before last year, I would never have imagined finding myself in a society where to say, "your butt is big," is to mean, "we like you," but I did. When such compliments were given, however true or false or in between they may have been, I smiled and blushed and the blush spilled down into the slight swagger in my hips and the bounce in my butt. And I admit it, after almost six months back in America, I still stick it out a little bit.

A native of Madison, Wisconsin, Wendy Soref recently graduated from Cornell University. On the heels of a nine-month stint in Dakar,

Senegal, she needed a truthful, satisfying medium to communicate her experiences abroad to the people in her life. With the encouragement of Professor Lydia Fakundiny, Ms. Soref found this medium in the travel essay. In the fall, she looks forward to plunging into her first year teaching second grade in Hughes, Arkansas.

*

I wouldn't say I'm a prude. I just don't like talking about body parts. I mean, there's really no need to mention the unmentionables, is there?

So imagine my surprise, nay, my horror, at my hands-on experience in a museum in Port Vila, Vanuatu. I was delightfully lost in the past, browsing with fascination the historical and traditional artifacts of the Ni-Vanuatu people. Here carefully woven baskets, there colorfully decorated fans. I was intrigued by everything I saw. Picking things up. Looking at them. Feeling how smooth or textured everything felt in my hands.

I came across a musical instrument, some kind of tribal horn. I picked it up and examined it. I raised it to my mouth, pursed my lips and blew. Nothing. Hmmm. I twisted it a little, and blew again, a little harder. Nothing. I heard some Islanders behind me giggling.

With the pride of Australia resting somewhere between my hands and my lips, I tried one more time to blow the instrument, to see what it sounded like. It can't be that hard. Come on, Aussie, come on! Still nothing.

"If at first you don't succeed, destroy all evidence that you tried." I was so out of there! As I hurriedly put the horn-like instrument back on the shelf, I noticed the tiny sign explaining what it was.

A small sign. With big bold letters.

PENIS GOURD.

Oh. My. God. I had been trying to "play" the penis gourd. In public. With my bare hands. Needless to say, as I backed out of the museum, babbling something about actually being a very *good* girl, the only thing I swallowed that day was my pride.

—Kirsty Olsen, "It's a What?"

* ✳ *

Tears from Turkey

She milks it in the time-honored way.

THERE WAS A TIME WHEN I PRIDED MYSELF FOR HAVING TEAR ducts of steel. I was the only kid on my block who could watch *Bambi* without bawling; *Beaches* made me snicker. Graduation. Weddings. Breakups. Disappointments. I endured it all with neither a sigh nor a whimper.

Until, that is, I went to Turkey.

Istanbul had been a destination point on my atlas for ages. After working in Beijing for a year, I finally made it, with loose plans of selling carpets by day and belly dancing at night. My plans changed my fifth day there, however, during a visit to the Archaeological Museum. As I gazed at a row of headless statues, my hand happened to brush against the spot on my thigh where I always strapped my money belt. Instead of a reassuring bundle, I felt only bare skin.

My heart stopped. I threw down my backpack, hiked up my ankle-length Guatemalan skirt, and gazed in horror.

The money belt was still there.

Its contents were not.

I stumbled about the museum in a state of shock. I had used my passport and American Express card only an hour before and deliberately sealed them both back into the belt. What happened? Did everything somehow fall out? How could I not have noticed? I remembered reading about thieves who tossed powder into tourists' eyes and robbed them blind in a matter of moments. Did that happen to me?

Panic set in as it dawned on me what I had just lost: money, credit cards, passport, airline ticket, traveler's checks, visa. In short, all forms of identity—except my Beijing work permit, which said I was American in Chinese—and all my finances, save for thirty dollars in Turkish lira.

I bolted for the museum's exit, nearly knocking over a museum guard in the process. "My passport!" I shrieked over my shoulder. I raced through Gulhane Park and the Topkapi Palace grounds, darting in and out of tourist patches, frantically retracing the casual stroll I had taken only minutes before. I was nearing the towering minarets of the Aya Sofya when I spotted a Turkish policeman. I scrambled over.

"I lost all my stuff!" I wailed.

He looked at me, amused. A couple of his buddies joined us.

"Money! Passport! Gone!" I told them.

One of the officers pointed with his rifle toward a building labeled "Tourism Police." I scurried over, dodged the security guard, and barged in on five officers settling down to an afternoon smoke.

Something I'd learned quickly on the road is that tactics differ from country to country. Vodka bribes had taken me far when I was an exchange student in Russia; I'd yelled a lot that past year in China. But what about Turkey?

When I approached the men with determination, not a one raised an eyebrow. Realizing that pushy women may not be well received in Turkey, I took a deep breath and tried reasoning with them.

They lit up another round of smokes.

I pleaded for their help.

One got up to make apple tea.

I was about to ask if they preferred Johnnie Walker Red Label or Black when I remembered that I was broke. I collapsed into a chair in despair, and—beyond my knowledge or control—a tear rolled down my cheek.

That did it.

I was instantly surrounded. One officer dabbed my eyes with a tissue; another handed me a phone. The third took to patting my shoulders and murmuring "No cry, no cry, no cry," while the fourth gave me some vital instructions: "You can get everything replaced as long as you say it was stolen. Understand? Not lost. Stolen." The fifth officer pounded away at a typewriter before handing me something written in Turkish that appeared important. With that, I was dismissed to the city police department.

I walked out of the building in a daze. I had never seen tears work outside of a B-grade movie. Surely Gloria Steinem would not have approved of what I just did. NOW would revoke my membership. I felt like a coward, an anti-feminist, the world's biggest wuss.

But then again, I was a wuss with an important-looking document in her hands on her way to the city police. I was going places.

I handed over the document with feigned confidence to the officer behind the desk. He looked it over carefully, eyebrows raised, before handing it to another officer, who walked it downstairs. I was wondering how someone could have possibly reached inside my money belt without my knowledge when a new police officer joined me. We made small talk for a couple of minutes—Where are you from? Texas? Do you have a horse?—before he stopped abruptly, looked straight into my soul, and said: "I saw you by the Aya Sofya. You said you *lost* your passport."

I tried not to blink. Was he bluffing? If not, should I? Then I had an idea.

"But all my stuff is gaaah-hnn," I blubbered as a fresh wave of tears dampened my streaked face.

Within five minutes, I had an official "Declaration of Theft" and directions to the American Consulate.

And then I just got shameless.

In the forty-eight hours that followed, I cried for the consulate and bawled for the bank. At first, I waited for a rejection before raising the floodgates. Then I got the tears flowing before I even walked through the door. My tear ducts got a little crusty, but I still managed some sobs for American Express. Not only was I ushered to the front of every line, but all emergency processing fees were summarily waived. My passport was replaced in three hours as opposed to three days; my traveler's checks were replaced in a matter of moments. The guys at the airline agency gave me a discount on my new ticket; a bank teller bought me lunch.

I never did figure out what happened to my money belt that day. But I've since learned that the Vietnamese sometimes hire professional criers for funerals.

I'm considering a career change.

Stephanie Elizondo Griest has belly danced with Cuban rumba queens, mingled with the Russian Mafiya, and edited the propaganda of the Chinese Communist Party. These adventures are the subject of her first book: Around the Bloc: My Life in Moscow, Beijing, and Havana. *She has also written for* The New York Times,

Washington Post, Latina Magazine, *and several Traveler's Tales anthologies. She once drove 45,000 miles across the nation in a beat-up Honda, documenting U.S. history for a website for kids on a fifteen-dollar daily budget. Visit her web site at www.aroundthebloc.com.*

✷

When planning any trip, the *most* important choice to make is buying *the* vacation purse. Oftentimes, a handbag is selected for its shape, color, or how well it goes as an accessory for one particular outfit. Forget that criteria! I need only to consider capacity and functionality. Whatever I think I need room for I must increase that estimate by 75 percent.

The most crucial feature of the prescribed handbag is an outside zippered compartment. It must be large enough to hold airline tickets, rail passes, passports, hotel confirmation slips, and rental car information. (This is just for the onset of the trip as more is added later.) There can be no hang-ups with this pouch as these documents must be accessible on demand. But in my case, having a husband who needs constant reassurance that nothing is lost or forgotten, these items must be checked, double-checked, and triple-checked daily. So the strength of the zipper is equally as important as the size of the compartment itself.

Now that I have placed my items inside the bag, it is time to include my husband's additions. I will need room for his cell phone, reading glasses, sunglasses, Palm Pilot, backup batteries for the cell phones, and a camera. As I look inside, it doesn't look too bad. I take the remaining space for the paperback that I want to read on the plane. All set!

As certain tourist meccas are notorious for thieves preying on the unsuspecting, the vacation purse needed to be less obvious. A suggestion was made to put the bag across my shoulder and wear my coat over top. After complying with this directive and seeing the results, this attempt to be circumspect was quickly abandoned. How discreet could I be with what looked like a sixty-pound tumor protruding from my left hip!

—Mona Cleary, "The Vacation Purse"

SUZANNE LAFETRA

* ✻ *

Hemorrhoids
in Holland

How do you say it in Dutch?

MY BRAND-SPANKING-NEW FIANCÉ HAD PLANNED THE details of an Amsterdam vacation. As our plane lifted us out of foggy San Francisco, he pressed his thigh into mine and I planned to launch us into monogamy with a big sexy bang. But after snuggling for fourteen hours, all the way to Schipol, my tush launched its own plan—one bad-ass hemorrhoid. My vacation fantasies dissolved in rectal ruin.

No romantic romp in a sunflower patch or playing footsie perched on the hard wooden stools of a local beer joint. No porn-style sexual hi-jinx while pigeons cooed outside our canal-side room. I imagined the perfect send off into the land of married life: kicking up our clogs along one of those dreamy canals, whispering sweet sensuous nothings awash in tulips, and no-holds-barred sexual gymnastics. But now instead of playing an adventuresome travel babe, kitten with a whip, and intimate soon-to-be wife rolled into one, I would probably lie in my hotel bed reading *Gone With the Wind*, alone.

Maybe it's not that big of a deal, I thought once we landed. I'll just run (or gingerly hobble) to the nearest pharmacy and pick up some medicine, and get right back into hottie mode. We could still lay the groundwork for a zesty marriage crammed with lots of lusty loving. We cruised through the narrow cobblestoned streets and I spotted a pharmacy.

But the shelves were lined with hundreds of identical white jars and tubes and boxes, all behind the counter. No familiar blue and yellow box of Preparation H within grabbing distance. I thought of our plans to bump along Dutch back roads atop quaint bicycles and winced. Then I approached the clerk who was standing behind the glass and quietly asked, "Do you carry Preparation H?"

The clerk cupped his hand to his ear. "Sorry?"

"Preparation H, please," I repeated. "For hemorrhoids." Between us was a thick pane of glass so it was necessary to project my voice rather loudly. There was a small hole cut into it at the absurdly inconvenient level of my left breast, so by crunching over and twisting my neck to the side I could speak directly into the empty circle. "I have a hemorrhoid and I need some medicine. Please."

The clerk was an intelligent-enough looking fellow, with wire-rimmed John Lennon-style glasses. He blinked through them at me and just shook his head.

I shifted, wishing I were back in my neighborhood drugstore, alone, and wearing a pair of my baggiest sweat pants. I glanced around. How many Amsterdam-ites were now aware of my problem? My fiancé thumbed through a men's magazine, probably revving up for a little afternoon delight. I sighed. We had not even been able to christen our hotel room with a round of jocular, newly-engaged lovemaking.

"Hem-orrh-oid creeeeam?" I tried again. Blank stare from the guy in the white coat.

My shoulders slumped. *I can't believe this.* Holland is a funky place, a loose, let-your-hair-down kind of place. You can fire up a joint in broad daylight, no questions asked. At the Sex Museum you can gawk at a photo of a donkey peeing into a woman's mouth. You can even admire the self-employed prostitutes waggling their wares in red-lighted windows. But finding a quick fix for hemorrhoids was tougher than scoring a hash brownie in the Oval Office.

"I have hemorrhoids," I said, even more forcefully, in the manner of an Ugly American who believes that the communication problem surely must lie with the dopey and deaf foreigner. My fiancé glanced over at me, and tucked the magazine back in the rack.

"My bottom hurts," I yelled, my nose and lips jammed through the hole in the glass. A snorting sound emerged from my soon-to-be husband. But just a head tilt and shoulder shrug from John Lennon.

I looked the clerk straight in the eye and made the same motion I had seen on TV: I held my hands about a foot apart, palms together, and squeezing them together said, *"Actually helps shrink swelling of hemorrhoidal tissues…"* A smile snuck onto my face. This whole thing was so bloody absurd!

My fiancé's chortling was not especially helpful as I tried to regain my composure, so I shot him what Mrs. Heimeral, my fourth grade teacher, had termed The Double Whammie Look, a piercing glance that could fizzle even the most potent eruption of giggles.

The clerk behind the glass was perhaps a relative of my old teacher—he was not laughing. He folded his arms, his mouth pressed in a grim line, and stared at the two Americans cluttering his shop. He had probably dealt with one too many stoned foreigners in his place of business.

"Please," I looked into his face. "I...I need, umm," I glanced around at the generic white containers. My fiancé must have sensed my growing desperation, because he cleared his throat, then came and put his arm around my shoulders, more or less straight-faced.

Suddenly, the white-coated chap held up his index finger, "Aaaaah!"

Thank you jeee-zus! I grinned in relief. I stood up tall and pulled a few bills from my pocket, tossing a victorious smile up at my fiancé.

The clerk turned around, white coat flapping, scanned the shelves and plucked something from the highest one. He faced us with a knowing wink and pushed a box of condoms across the counter.

My partner turned away in a fit of snorting. Deflated, I imagined meals consisting mostly of prunes and scoring a big fat *zero* on the vixen scale.

I glanced around to see if there was anyone else in the store. The only person was my lover, now a hunched hee-hawing man over whom the Double Whammie was powerless.

Oh, what the hell. I certainly wasn't going to get any *more* embarrassed. I took a deep breath. I bent over, with my bum toward the pharmacist, and pointed straight to the offending location. And then, quickly uprighting myself, I squinted and pinched my eyebrows together and proclaimed a theatrical, exaggerated "Owwww!"

Just to make sure he was getting it, I twirled around a second time and repeated the pained face while gesturing at my ailing arse.

High-pitched wheezing sounds emerged from my fiancé

as he pounded out of the store, setting the little bell on the door to jangling furiously. He was still wiping his eyes a few minutes later when I triumphantly strutted—well, minced—out clutching a little white bag containing a tube of Dutch Preparation H, which, in case you ever need to know, is called Spurti.

My tissues did eventually shrink. After we gently made love I stroked my fiancé's strong, freckled shoulder while the carillon bells rippled through the city. The rest of our pre-marital vacation brimmed with sensual pleasures, even though most of them didn't involve the Kama Sutra and KY Jelly. We drank in the garish colors of van Gogh and wept as we squatted in Anne Frank's tiny hiding place. One frigid night we dipped our fingers in the cold Amstel River and roamed for hours until we found a seventeenth-century pub and filled our bellies with perfect skunky beer. On our last afternoon in the Netherlands, we fantasized about moving to Amsterdam—the skinny building where we might live, the flower vendor we'd become friendly with, the Rembrandt paintings we'd pore over with our children. The dominatrix spanking fantasy paled in comparison.

We did have to make one more trip back to that pain-in-the-ass pharmacy though. But that time we had no trouble getting what we needed—just a few more condoms.

Suzanne LaFetra has settled into a comfy marriage with her former boyfriend, and rarely ventures into foreign pharmacies these days. She is an award-winning writer whose work has appeared in magazines, newspapers, and literary publications. She lives in Berkeley with her husband and two children.

*

I had just arrived in Korea on a one-year contract to teach English. I was assigned to teach the early evening classes because I was the newcomer and all the other Canadian instructors preferred a day-time schedule.

My first evening on the job, my Korean male colleague came up to me, introduced himself and asked if I had eaten dinner yet. I told him I hadn't and after he took a long pause and looked down at the floor for a while, he asked if I would have dinner with him. I thought how sweet it was that he was so shy to ask me out, and he seemed even more shy as the night went on from the way he rarely spoke and rushed through our dinner.

At the end of my second day teaching, another Korean male colleague came up to me, asked me a question about English grammar and asked if I had eaten dinner yet. When I mentioned I hadn't had dinner, he asked me to join him, and like the colleague the night before, rushed through his dinner and seemed in a hurry to leave.

I wasn't surprised on my third evening teaching when another male colleague asked me if I had had dinner and then suggested we go out to eat.

Later that night I called my friend in Canada who had worked in Korea the year before, to tell her what a big hit I was in Korea—that I had been asked out every night by a different man.

When I mentioned how shy they all were, and started by asking if I had eaten dinner as their opening line—she told me that in Korea the greeting, "Hello. How are you?" can't be translated, and the Korean greeting is actually, "Hello. Have you eaten dinner?"

She went on to tell me that not only is it rude for me to say I hadn't eaten dinner, but also that the men asking me had to bring me out to eat by Korean etiquette!

—Melissa H. M. Valks, "All in a Manner of Speaking"

DEBORAH J. SMITH

* * *

A Tale of
Two Churches

Was she forgiven, or what?

I skipped the Penance Service for Lent. I don't count myself among the Unforgiven. I've painted myself into an impossible corner: I wouldn't confess to the priests I know because they know me too well. But I found out it's a disaster telling your sins to a stranger.

At Saint Peter's in Rome, there were lines for individual confession. I'd read an essay extolling the virtues of confession at St. Peter's. In a moment I can only credit to madness, I thought, "Why not?"

It was forever since I'd last gone to confession—but I had *not* committed murder, robbery, infidelity, or child abuse in any fashion. With those off the playing field, everything seemed innocent enough. I grabbed my parcels and got in the line.

I never do things the easy way. Forgetting that Vatican City is a hotbed of religious conservatives, I also forgot my best shot was the Japanese-speaking priest. I kept on looking for one who spoke English. I was doomed.

After "Bless Me Father," I said it was years since my last

confession. The priest asked *why* I was away so long? (Note to priests: Want the penitent to return again? Try congratulating her on having the courage to be here in the first place.) He said he'd just go down the Ten Commandments and ask me about them.

Without trying to blaspheme, the Ten Commandments are rife with Sins for the Unsuspecting. I can't imagine Moses going down the mountain with them and not interrupting God a few times—wanting to know exactly what God meant by this one or that one in terms of daily Hebrew life. Suddenly, a noise broke into my Biblical daydream.

"Did you take God's name in vain?" the priest asked.

Jesus Christ! is the typical exclamation of Irish people (and me) when frustrated, surprised, or amazed. It's usually not said as a prayer.

"Did I say 'Jesus Christ!' when I wasn't praying? Of course; I'm Irish." My humor sailed right past him. This was the second commandment.

Questions continued—something about excessive drinking, which led me to recall a night in Washington, D.C. when my best friends, also well oiled, caught me before I fell down the subway stairs. That spoke of loyalty and compassion, but I was pressed further about the number, kind, and frequency of my spiritual failings. I was bothered by this questioning without context, with no consideration of my reasons or my life. How do I own the spiritual consequences of my decisions without someone judging me?

I wasn't planning on offering excuses anyway. I'm glad there are only ten commandments, not twenty or thirty.

We were knee-deep into "Thou shalt not kill." I had an informed conscience and an American accent. Use your imagination to figure out the topic. The portrait of me now—flitting across my mind's eye—was a drunk who swore and beat her family. I thought suddenly: this skewed picture just isn't me.

In the cold light of this new perspective my personal, examined morals seemed less and less a part of the priest's business. So when he asked me point blank what I did about the particulars, I used a point-blank solution. Praying intently to God, I lied.

Lied.

Now I had crossed a new threshold for transgressions: a Third Dimension in Sin. What happens when you lie in confession?

Funny though, what a sense of humor God really has…two minutes later, the priest asked me if I'd ever lied.

Quickly I replied: "Yes, I did." Whoa!

"How many times?"

I stared at the wavy glass in the confessional and crossed my eyes. More lies now? No, no…wait, random numbers! I haven't kept track since forever, remember?

Now penance? Would I have to impale myself on a Swiss Guard's spear? Or could I negotiate for a root canal without anesthesia? That fellow who wrote about the spiritual boost he got from confession at Saint Peter's? I'm convinced he's a lunatic.

As entertaining as these thoughts were, my blood ran cold when I couldn't remember the Act of Contrition at the end. This is the truth: I can *always* remember the first line. My high school teacher, Fr. Jim Hartley, would say, "Oh my God, I am heartily sorry…I'm Hartley, hey God, remember me?" as the class groaned at the pun. Thirty years later, I always got the first line, but after that? Nothing. I'd forgotten.

His voice wavering with frustration, the priest asked if I was sorry for my sins.

"Yes."

"Do you resolve not to do them again?"

"Yes." Oh please, oh please, oh please…. My hands were like ice. It was close to ninety degrees that day in Rome. I thought of sunshine outside.

"Say ten Hail Marys." The priest launched into Absolution; he wasn't looking to prolong this either.

Outside in the Basilica, I felt like I'd been a player in a video game. All I could do was dive through moral loopholes. Oddly, I wasn't feeling guilty.

Was I in denial? Was my life as terrible as it sounded? Most importantly, were my sins *really forgiven*, even if I'd lied and then (truthfully) admitted so? Every question had been formulated to catch me in sin, not help me see the love of God. I'm old enough to face my failings; but I swore to myself I wouldn't be caught in a setup like that one again.

I was off confession permanently. My penance, along with ten Hail Marys, came when I left my parcels behind in the Box. I had to get back in line to retrieve them.

A year later, the good Sisters in Assisi asked if I'd like to go to their Penance Service for Ash Wednesday. I politely declined, mentioning I'd gone to confession at Saint Peter's. Had to give up *something* for Lent.

But at a nearby college during this Lenten season, when talk centered on the parable of the Prodigal Son, the matter took a different turn.

For those who aren't familiar with the parable, here's a quick version:

The youngest son of a wealthy man grabs his share of the family fortune and heads out to see the world. This adventure fuels his wild living and loose women by the score—until his money runs out. Then youngest son is forced to take an underrated service job slopping pigs for market. In the midst of work, the son realizes his father's servants have a better life than this. He quits and heads home to talk his way into becoming one of Dad's hired hands.

Meanwhile, the eldest son is home doing his bit with Dad. The father has resigned himself to his youngest being dead in a big-city gutter. So you can imagine how thrilled the father is one day, when he looks over the countryside to see Youngest son coming down the road towards home.

Dad gets more than excited—he throws a big bash to celebrate his son who was lost, but now found. This is all going swimmingly, especially for youngest son, until the eldest brother asks Dad why he never celebrated anything with him, even though he's done what the father wanted all these years? And eldest son has the party details—one of the servants told all.

Dad's reply? All you had to do was ask, Sonny Boy. In the meantime, someone we thought was dead is alive. Good reason for a party if you ask me.

The college discussion started out trying to examine which character in the story each person could identify with. It rapidly evolved into an examination of character portrayal in the parable. The entire interaction said lots about each contributor's individual orientation to people, a fact I quietly chose to keep to myself.

The priest in the discussion would like to have been the all-forgiving, compassionate father. But he just couldn't see himself really doing it. He also thought the eldest brother picked the sleazy servant who was the House Tattler, so he'd get all the details of the homecoming party for his younger brother.

One of the students insisted it wasn't this way, that the eldest son bullied the servant into forking over the party details. Maybe, she insisted, it was the desperate act of hired help cornered by the boss. Hey, we've all been *there*.

Truth is, the Prodigal Son is an allegory of God's love for us, about love without limits and second chances, given in the most unlikely of circumstances. Some call this foolishness and cheap grace, but it says much about what unconditional love really will do.

Later, I thought about it more. Fried to within an inch of my life, I swore off confession, an endurance test for me at the best of times, for the rest of my days. Or, as my husband likes to say, until the next time…when the grass is green, the sun sets over the hill, and the moon is full…

In Italy with my young son this year, I found myself riding the bus at the day's end, down the hills past the green fields of Assisi towards the Basilica of Santa Maria degli Angeli. This Basilica was built over the Porziuncola, a tiny chapel where St. Francis worshiped with the early friars and accepted St. Clare as one of his own. The place where St. Francis died is also nearby. I hadn't taken the time to see it on previous trips.

Entering the Basilica, I saw the lights and asked my son if he wanted to go to confession. He declined, indicating he goes when his Catholic school at home takes him there. I was off the hook; this forgiveness thing was behind me, too.

Even as light fades and the night approaches, the Porziuncola remains the central feature shining in the middle of the Basilica. I approached the entry and stood with the others who were there to pray, thinking of Francis and how different life must have been when all this was woodland and fields, a simple stone church with friars camping outside and everyone living in poverty. For St. Francis, this was his home. I offered a prayer or two, and read the Latin inscription along the doorstep: "Here is Holy."

My son dragged me over to an audio guide and asked me to put in a euro. We shared earphones as we listened to the story of the church and watched the light change in the Basilica with the coming of the evening. The Catholic Church, said the audioguide, grants forgiveness of all one's sins as an indulgence to those who visit the Porziuncola to pray.

I was stunned. After the grandiose hair-splitting at the Vatican, here in the quiet simplicity of this chapel, my sins were simply forgiven? To my mind an even, decent trade—a rarity in life. Although that wasn't the reason for my visit, like the youngest son in the parable, I wouldn't decline the offer either.

Call it foolishness or cheap grace if you like. As the sun slipped away and the moon rose over the hill town of Assisi, I stumbled onto an earthier, more compassionate kind of Christianity. It didn't deny responsibility, good works, or belief, but as I always knew, my life needn't be lived as a moral loophole. Rather than engineering faith, perhaps it was a second chance given from unconditional love.

Or maybe I am more like the prodigal son than I care to know.

Deborah J. Smith is a faculty member at Empire State College in Saratoga Springs, New York. A contributing writer for Tastes of Italia *magazine, her work also airs on NorthEast Public Radio. She will return again to Italy—four years of high school Latin won't go to waste—and remain Catholic for the foreseeable future.*

* ✻ *

The Mile-High and Dry Club

Everyone wants the right (seat) mate.

"HI," HE SAID. HE WAS ADORABLE, AND HE APPEARED TO have the seat next to mine on the plane. That never happens. I usually end up sitting next to someone with a child, which means either making silly faces for five hours or appearing to be a woman who doesn't like children. I do like children. I want to have some eventually. I just don't want to fly with them.

In fact, I have no political aspirations, but I did once come up with what I think is an excellent program to keep teenage girls from getting pregnant. Give them a baby (preferably one with an earache) for the duration of a cross-country flight. The child's parents could sit in another row and enjoy a little break, the teenager could fly free (an incentive for the teenager and the parents), and the teen pregnancy rate would plummet. It's a good idea, don't you think? If anybody in elected office or in charge of an airline is reading this book, it's yours. All I ask is that you get this program in place before I have a child.

I am somewhat chastised, because last time I flew, I was

looking forward to sleeping on the plane, and a woman with a screaming baby got on board and I was thinking, "Please don't let that baby be sitting next to me, please don't let that baby be sitting next to me," and of course, he was sitting next to me. And this baby looked healthy, like he could scream all the way to L.A. and back. His weary mother dropped off a baggie of Cheerios and then looked for an empty overhead compartment in which to put, I hoped, the baby. I took this opportunity to surreptitiously summon a flight attendant, and said that if another seat opened up, I would very much like to move. She nodded sympathetically. Then the woman sat down, let out a big sigh and said, "It's so hard to travel with a baby. When I was pregnant everybody was so nice, and now it's like I'm a pariah." I instantly felt guilty, and overcompensated by pretending to be equally indignant: "It's true. It's a disgrace. Everybody was a baby once. Why aren't people more tolerant?" I spent the rest of the flight praying the flight attendant would *not* offer me the seat I requested. In fact, I felt so remorseful and hypocritical that by the time we were somewhere over Phoenix I was holding the Cheerios and singing "The Itsy Bitsy Spider."

So it was particularly refreshing and startling to see an adorable man about to sit next to me, and even more refreshing to hear him say, "Hi." I was well into visions of the two of us joining the Mile-High Club when I realized he was speaking: "Would you mind switching seats so I can sit with my girlfriend, Candi?" Candi looked at me sweetly. She was predictably blond and thin. O.K., first of all, her name was Candi, so I didn't like her already. Second of all, he didn't *have* to say her name, so obviously he just enjoyed saying it, enjoyed dating a Candi. Third of all, Candi stole my man. And fourth of all (am I allowed four?), I wasn't feeling very supportive of relationships. So I said that. I actually said, "You know, I just broke up with someone, and I'm not feeling very *pro-love* right now, so if you don't mind, I really don't want to switch seats." Candi looked disappointed. I felt like a raving bitch. But I held my ground (and my window seat) because why was I singled out to move? I'll tell you why. Because I'm single! I can sit anywhere! Nobody will miss me!

Candi and her boyfriend smiled at each other wistfully and shrugged. How would they survive apart? Not my problem. I was alone. I was going home for the holidays alone. I had to find a space in long-term parking alone and lug my bags alone to the bus stop alone and take them off the bus alone and wait in the line alone to check in alone, and when I got to my sister's house in Dallas, I would be sleeping on a futon in the baby's room alone. So I figured Candi could be alone for one fucking flight.

——) ——

Our second night back in Paris, we woke to the unmistakable sound of enthusiastic, extended copulation. The acoustics of the airshaft were such that our neighbors' every gasp and groan reverberated with crystal clarity. We lay rigid in our beds, my mother and I, unable to ignore what was happening so bright, early, and close at hand. I couldn't help observing that at least someone was getting her money's worth out of a Paris hotel room. She vocalized without inhibition, as people do when their mothers aren't within earshot. I wondered if she was a pro. "Sounds like a chicken," Mom observed grimly, staring at the ceiling.

◆

—Ayun Halliday,
No Touch Monkey

Her boyfriend turned out to be a very nice guy. We talked the whole way to Dallas. And we didn't talk about her. She was barely a blip on our radar. When he asked me for a pen, I knew Candi was on the way out. He would give me his number and we would end up together, and the whole thing would make a great story, all because I wouldn't give up my seat.

He wrote "I love you" on his cocktail napkin (which I thought seemed a little premature!) and then he had the people in front of us pass the note to Candi.

How many people must be inconvenienced by this relationship?

As he gave me back my pen, I wished I were sitting next to a screaming baby.

Cindy Chupack was a writer/executive producer of HBO's Sex and the City. *Her work on the show earned her several Emmy and Golden Globe awards. She has written for a number of television shows, including* Everybody Loves Raymond, *and for several magazines, including* Glamour, *where she had her own column. This story was excerpted from her first book,* The Between Boyfriends Book. *She lives in New York City and Los Angeles.*

* ✶ *

Blame It on Rio

She needed a job below the equator.

I WOULD *NEVER* HAVE DONE IT AT HOME.

I could blame it on peer pressure, curiosity or kink, but deep down, I know it's the road. Travel, whether to summer camp or Sri Lanka, has a way of making previously unthinkable activities seem not only normal but logical, desirable. Something about travel unlocks the secrets I don't even tell myself, the wishes I'm unaware of until I've granted them.

In my real life, I am Midwestern. Middle-aged. Married. But on the road, I'm a woman who takes risks and sends postcards. *"Ran a roadblock in Rome." "Ate a bug in Chiang Mai." "Got up close and personal with a cobra in Putra Jaya. Wish you were here."*

And that's how I came to be here. Doing this.

In retrospect, it's almost exactly like losing your virginity. You remember the first time you even heard about it. That squinty girl—the one who took your lunch last winter— starts whispering in gym. They do *what* to you? Oh my God. They do not.

She nods, smirking at your ignorance. They do. And it hurts. I've done it. Everyone has done it. You'll do it, too.

But you won't. Never. Not as long as you live.

You try to put it and the squinty girl out of your head. Her lunch-thieving ways are only tolerated because she's always been first. White leather go-go boots, in second grade. Her mother's cigarettes, a few years later. She'll grow up to drink the first Cosmopolitan. But surely, she's lying.

She's not. And now that you know about it, it's everywhere. An awful lot of people are doing it. Even some of your friends.

"It only really hurts the first time."

"The boys like it. A lot."

"Have a few drinks first. It makes it easier."

The realization, of course, hits you on the road. You find yourself one morning in Manhattan and you realize that everybody is doing it. Has done it, and you've been left behind.

You are the last woman in America with pubic hair, and it must go.

This is how I wound up flat on my back, a thousand miles from home, with a complete stranger painting electric blue wax over the part of me that is best referred to as "down there." This is no itsy-bitsy teeny-weeny bikini wax—and I've never had one of those before. This is a Brazilian. It's the full monty, the Roman orgy of hair removal services.

New York is the obvious place to do it. People in my hometown know quite enough about me. And if things turn out badly, I can always lie. "I did not. I was there for a *conference.*" Like a Canadian boyfriend, a weekend in New York can be anything you want it to be.

I choose Bliss because frankly, if I've heard of them way out in the Heartland, they must be good. And Bliss uses some kind of secret mojo wax, an aromatherapy-based potion from Australia that promises to be pain-free. I don't believe it, but I'm reassured, anyway.

Reassured, that is, until Claudia leads me into the "treatment room," and I see the oxygen tank. Before I can flee, she explains that the tank is for "oxygen facials," and that I won't be needing resuscitation. Claudia is a tiny cheerful brunette who looks nineteen but says she's thirty. They're doing something right here, anyway.

"You promise it won't hurt?" Great. I'm squeaking. She looks nineteen and I sound twelve.

Claudia shrugs. "It's much, much better than the old waxes. But it depends on your pain tolerance, I guess."

When it comes to pain, I am a complete…oh, never mind. Claudia offers me paper panties (for modesty?) but says it's easier to wax without them. If I was that shy, I wouldn't be here. So I shed the slacks, climb up on the table and take a couple of deep breaths. Let the loss begin.

O.K., that wax is *hot*. I whimper and Claudia realizes she has a problem child on her hands. "We don't have to take it all off," she offers. "A lot of women leave a little…landing strip."

I've been thinking that completely bare is sort of pervy even for me, so I agree to this instantly. Claudia keeps talking and applying the wax, while I try to settle down. The music here is good—Van Morrison and Warren Zevon instead of that New Age crap you hear in most spas. In the ninth circle of Hell, you pay fifty bucks to have your pubes ripped out while Enya caterwauls for all eternity.

Aiyeeeeeee. Van Morrison was distracting me, but now it's showtime. Claudia works quickly, pulling fast and then pressing her fingers over the area to help stop the stinging. I wonder (aloud) if anyone has ever flipped right off this table. She says no, but I can tell she's thinking there's a first time for everything. I should have listened to the girls and had a margarita.

I should have stayed home.

The pain, quantifiably, is about that of your worst band-aid experience, cubed. The whole procedure takes fifteen minutes. Two minutes of that is pure torture, but it's spread out in three-second increments throughout the wax. Claudia tells me I'm doing pretty well.

It's over more quickly than I thought it would be. Claudia and I thank each other, awkwardly, and then she leaves. I wonder if she'll talk about me to the other waxers tomorrow. There's no mirror, so I grab my compact and examine her handiwork. It looks very…kempt.

Leaving, I catch my reflection in a storefront window. I'm walking differently. There's a tiny, knowing smirk around my lips. I realize, with certainty, that I'll be doing this again. But first I need to find three things: A boy. White boots. And a postcard.

Cynthia Barnes has interviewed Billy Bob Thornton for Premiere, *judged apple pie for* Slate, *and tagged along on an archaeological dig for* National Geographic. *When she's not scuba diving in Borneo for* Endless Vacation *or rating romantic spas for* Continental, *she's at work on her first book,* Blue Wanders From Arkansas to Timbuktu. *She has received an NEA grant for fiction and is a Ragdale fellow. Cynthia's adventures are chronicled at www.cynthiabarnes.com.*

ANNIE CAULFIELD

* * *

Don't Slap the Witchdoctor

The strange ways of the bush are alive and well.

"THIS IS WHERE THE POLITICIAN EXPLODED." ISIDORE WAVED a hand at the town sign. "*Paf!* And gone."

I thought he was talking about a bomb.

Benin had violently changed governments nine times in twelve years during the nervy, bad old days between 1960 and 1972. One political hopeful declared himself president at nine in the morning and was gone by teatime. Running Benin was no job for anyone looking for a good night's sleep, a pension plan, or a long life—until President Kérékou came along in 1972 and showed how a tough guy with a heavily scarred face, and no qualms about house smashings or random arrests, could keep himself in charge for a very long time. Yet even under Kérékou's stern regime, coup enthusiasts made sure no more than three years passed without running, shouting, shooting, and bleeding outside the presidential palace, right up until the late nineties. So when I heard talk of exploded politicians, a bomb did seem likely.

"Who blew him up?"

Isidore looked at me, then quickly back at the road—in these country towns a chicken or a child could be darting recklessly in front of the car at any moment. "In fact," he said, "he did it himself."

"An accident?"

Regardless of small darting perils on the road, Isidore had to look at me again. As always, impatience was tempered to a long-suffering weariness, the way the good-natured remind themselves not to snap at the slow-witted—just take a deep breath and try to communicate, yet again.

"How could it be an accident? You know the story?"

"No."

"No. So how can you talk of an accident when you're hearing this for the first time?"

I said nothing. Isidore drove on a while, composing his thoughts for the storytelling, steeling himself to deal with further treacle-headed incomprehension, bound to spoil things before his punchline if he didn't keep strict control of the conversation.

Apparently some people can do that thing where you hire a taxi driver and you're in charge of things. I'm sure I've done it myself on a number of occasions, but not with Isidore. With Isidore, I paid him, but if I proved unable to meet the standards he required of a passenger, I could find myself put out at a roadside anywhere in Benin's 113,000 square kilometers, an area slightly smaller than England but inconveniently hot and unfamiliar for the sudden pedestrian.

Isidore told me what time he'd collect me, where I'd be going, what to learn from the journey, and where I'd be staying at its end. He told me what to eat, when to eat it, and how much water to drink with and between these meals. If I didn't eat enough, or drink the right gallonage of water, I'd be firmly scolded. And sleep? If I didn't sleep enough, well, that was just pushing Isidore to the limits of his tolerance.

It was no good for me to insist that I didn't usually sleep much; Isidore simply wasn't having an ill-rested passenger in his car. He reintroduced me to the concept of the afternoon nap, not something I'd taken since the age of four. It was no use for me to imagine that now that I was closing in on four-zero I might be old enough to know my own sleep requirements. Isidore was as dogmatic on the nap subject as my nap-insisting granny had been— and he didn't even bother bribing me with a Wagon Wheel.

"Listen, we've had a busy morning. There are things to see later, when it's cool, so if you don't sleep now you'll be destroyed for them. I'll be back at six. Wake up at five-thirty, shower and change so you'll be fresh for the next events."

"But…"

After the first defeat over nap time, I still had a spark of rebellion left in me. When Isidore returned on the dot of six, triumphantly crowing that I looked wonderfully refreshed, I told him that I'd not actually slept, just lain on my bed reading. He frowned and sighed. The following day when I was sent to my hotel after lunch, he said: "And make sure you sleep. Don't read."

I lied after that, told him I had marvelous deep dreams, cat-on-the-mat luxuriant afternoon sleeps—because you can keep disobeying your granny and she'll forgive you, but Isidore…he didn't need to be doing with the likes of me. He could go back to the taxi drivers' off-season state of having no passengers at all; hanging around outside a hotel in Cotonou, Benin's non-official capital, for fareless hours on end, his bills at home mounting up, the family larder running low—anything was better than ferrying about some substandard passenger in his carefully preserved, hand-painted, glowing turquoise 1980 Peugeot.

So, by day five, I knew an exploded-politician story was best left to be told and not interrupted with foolish questions from someone who would surely be thinking more clearly had she really had her full nap time as instructed.

"As a young politician from the south went north to talk to the people...I'm speaking slowly so you understand."

I nodded. Isidore knew my grasp of French could be wayward. This was one reason he felt I should have constant stern supervision—as a woman who'd come alone to Benin, with such a comically bizarre command of the country's only European language, I was obviously not the full franc piece.

"The politician went around telling people they should vote for him. People said yes, yes, of course, the way people do to make a politician go away. But then he went to see a very old man, who said to him: 'I don't trust you young people of today.' Then the old man turned his back and started smoking his pipe.

"Very angry, the young politician slapped his face—'You listen to me,' he said.

"The old man kept on smoking his pipe. 'You shouldn't have slapped me,' he said.

"The politician laughed. 'Ha! You're an old man, what are you going to do about it?' And he slapped him again!

"The old man just said quietly, 'You'll be sorry you did that.'

"The young politician laughed even harder and drove away in his limousine.

"On his way home, the hand he'd used for slapping started to swell up. Then the whole arm swelled, swelled up like a balloon. Then his other hand and the other arm swelled. Swelled so he couldn't drive anymore. Someone from a village had to take him home and all the way back he kept swelling—one leg, two legs, neck, stomach, back…all. They took him to the hospital.

"'Ah no,' said the doctor. 'We can't cure this with hospital medicine. You need a *guérisseur*.' Annie, you know *guérisseur?*"

I was alert. I did. *Guérisseur*, traditional healer, practitioner of the shamanic magic arts of *gri-gri*.

"The *guérisseur* came to the hospital and said, 'Yes, this is *gri-gri*. But it's too strong for me. Only the person who put this on you can take it away.'

"The old man from the north was sent for. He said he would have lifted the *gri-gri* if it was up to him, but it was his father who did it, and his father had died twenty-one years ago. He'd sent the *gri-gri* from beyond the grave. So there was nothing to be done. The young politician went on swelling—legs, head, back, front…. He swelled until he died of it, exploded like a balloon all over the hospital."

I laughed. "That'll teach him."

"It teaches him nothing." Isidore scowled at me. "He is dead. But us, we should learn from it. Don't be horrible to anyone in this life, slapping them and such, because they might have more power than you think."

The politician exploded by *gri-gri* was only one verse in Isidore's unabridged head-bible of *gri-gri* stories. Crooked policemen were chased by *gri-gri* bees, bandits were pursued by the lizards of *gri-gri* justice, and politicians…. It seemed they barely had a moment's peace to enjoy power before entering the records as yet another example of the particular *gri-gri* vulnerability of their profession. Not that they didn't deserve it. One politician, having stolen tax money from many vil-lagers, had been *gri-gri*-ed into flinging himself from a fast-moving car in the prime of his health and was immediately stone-dead in the road. This one sounded like an assassination cover story to me, but the alleged power of *gri-gri* to strike a politician on behalf of the average Beninois Joe must have been a comfort in a country where "politician" was a word often interchangeable with "thief" or "thug."

Thieves and thugs had severely disrupted Isidore's child-hood. His father, a respected healer and *gri-gri* practitioner, had been forced to spend years away from the family village, hiding from political whim that could have resulted in imprisonment or execution.

In the early seventies, the newly installed young Marxist-Leninist dictator, Mathieu Kérékou, decided to shake up the power that the magic men held in rural communities. There were harassments, arrests, shrine desecrations…Benin would be sort of Chinese, Cuban, North Korean and, a bit made up by Kérékou, socialist modern. Benin would also be Benin; because, until 1975, it had been something else.

When people asked me where I was talking about, where I was going on my travels with Isidore, I had to remember that the state I was trying to know was not well known, nor was it the place that people who thought they knew, knew.

"The little thin place here on the map between Togo and Nigeria," I'd tell the completely Benin blank-minded, finding the atlas page for them.

"It's shaped like a willy," they'd say.

"Well, there's nothing I can do about that," I'd say.

And I couldn't do a great deal for the better informed, who'd start talking about ancient African empires and fantastic Benin bronzes in the British Museum—I had to cut them short—tell them they were talking about the wrong place.

I had suspicious thoughts about why, very soon after first meeting me, Isidore continually emphasized the blessings that could be bestowed on women who got themselves involved with a Beninois man who had easy access to gynecological *gri-gri*. White women, that is. Story after story of lonely white women of a certain age, saved by a combination of *gri-gri* and youthful Beninois male vigor. The white woman was always rich, the man strong, handsome, and desperately poor. A bit like Isidore.

Isidore's favorite white-woman story was definitely a thing of inexplicable wonder. There was a French woman, forty years old. Her husband had died after twenty years of mar-

---

I met Gianpiero on the Inca Trail. He was Italian, thirty-six, tall, dark, and handsome. He spoke Italian, and…Italian.

After the trek, we gave up on talking, took up smooching, and decided to travel to northern Peru together.

Well, girls, we can all imagine the advantages of not being able to communicate with our man. But when you mix a fiery Italian temperament with a back-talking New Yorker, you simply can't get the two to shut up.

And oh, how we argued! Or, tried to argue. Believe me, there are few things more ridiculous than two people trying to argue in disparate languages, pausing every few words to look something up in their dictionaries.

◆

—Amy Tobey, "How to Speak Italian in Spanish"

riage to her; they had no children and her heart was broken. When she came to Benin on holiday she seldom went on excursions with her friends, just sat alone on the beach reading magazines. A young man saw her there every day. He was very young, just eighteen. He asked her why she was always sad and she told him her story—told him how her situation wouldn't be so miserable if she'd been able to have a child, but she'd had two miscarriages and her doctors said childbearing was impossible for her now. The young man talked to her at length and promised her that, if she had a baby with him, they could go to his uncle who did *gri-gri* and the baby would be fine. The French woman liked the young man and decided to take the risk. The uncle gave her an infusion to drink before sex with the young man. She did what she was asked and she became pregnant. The woman had to remain in Benin in the constant care of the *gri-gri* uncle; he gave her infusions to drink and potions to wash with during every day of her pregnancy. The baby was born healthy. She went back to France, taking with her her thriving child and the young man. It turned out, she wasn't just quite a rich woman—she was a member of the Peugeot family and incredibly rich. The young man never had to do a stroke of work again, sent presents to all his family, and returned to Benin only for holidays, staying in the Sheraton Hotel with the millionaires.

"They are both happy," Isidore concluded. "Through sheer luck, both have what they wanted, both are happy."

I think Isidore told me these stories hoping that I'd spread the word to single white females back home, having quickly established that I wasn't up for participation in such happiness myself. He'd offered it to me within thirty seconds, jumping out of his car when he saw me sitting on a hotel terrace in

Cotonou. Not the Sheraton Hotel for millionaires, but a government-run collapse of a place on the beachfront. Very Graham Green, very hard to get a drinkable cup of coffee. Very few nights when the water or the electricity weren't cut, very few mornings when seeing the spray of Atlantic breakers behind coconut palms as I came down the chipped stone stairs to breakfast didn't make me catch my breath with excitement. No day that starts with a chokingly great view can end that badly. No proposal of marriage made within thirty seconds can end well.

Isidore had asked me how I liked Benin so far, asked me my age, nationality and if I was traveling alone.

"Alone? Good. I am very interested in European women. English is better for me than French, nicer people. I'm thirty-four, only a bit younger than you. It's ideal, we can marry."

His medium-height stockiness and military type of hold on himself were contradicted by lash-flickered pretty eyes and perfectly shaped, high-arched brows, like he'd stolen them from Lauren Bacall. His smile was as reassuring as a big, firm handshake. But it wasn't ideal. I invented a live-in, long-standing boyfriend fretting at home.

"I see. You really like him?"

"We'll get married next year."

"O.K. Well, you'll need a taxi driver anyway. Don't speak to any other driver but me. I'm the best."

As we went on our first short journey around town, to track down where exactly Sabena Airlines and Air Afrique had decided between themselves to send my luggage other than Cotonou, Isidore told me he wasn't seriously expecting marriage. He had just wanted to put forward a future possibility. I suggested that this still wasn't a sensible way to go about things—people needed more time to get to the future-possibility stage.

"But now I know there is no future possibility, that issue is closed, there's no time wasted. Do you want to buy trousers here?"

I was boiling in jeans and couldn't wait till my bags reappeared to find something cooler to wear. Along the main boulevard of Cotonou women used the roadside trees as high, flapping showrooms for locally made clothes—very cheap and on the noisy edge of cheerful. Isidore bargained some bellowing loud giraffe-print trousers down out of a tree for me. I decided there was no point paying more for something that looked less clownish when my own quiet trousers should be only a few hours away. Actually they were still in Belgium and, due to some airline-staff determination to keep the old jokes about lost baggage alive and uproarious, they would arrive with me, via Cameroon, in four days' time.

The four days gave me the opportunity to decide how I felt about the future possibility of Isidore as a taxi driver to the more remote parts of Benin. By the time I was wearing my own trousers, I knew. As much as you can know if it's wise to put your time in someone else's hands.

As we progressed through the country, Isidore constantly bossing, storytelling, and explaining, I was glad he didn't ask me any more about my home life—I could have forgotten details of my made-up fiancé and been caught out. But there was still a worry: what if we bumped into Isidore's father and his metalworking magic sussed me out as a fraud, a free, single woman who, if far from having access to Peugeot-type bank accounts, was still relatively wealthy and going to waste?

Scrupulously honest Isidore would certainly have found my big lie to him a sackable offense in a passenger.

Maybe it's not an unembellished truth that he'd have to put me out at a remote roadside, a passenger without references, had I failed to comply with his requirements of an employer; but it would have been all too easy to destroy the comfortable dynamic of our relationship with more subtle offenses than outright lies to him. As with most comfortable things—armchairs, for instance—it could be a small complaint, like a loose tiny wing nut, that could send everyone sprawling to the floor hurt and embarrassed.

Isidore had created the dynamic. He knew where potential loose tiny wing nuts could be, so he liked every choice I made to be referred to him. Even my choice of bathroom facility.

"If you really need to go, go, but it's not clean. Better to go in a field later."

Deciding this was one subject I didn't need to discuss with him wouldn't do either.

"You don't piss? It's been three hours. Are you sick?"

"I went in the museum toilets; I just didn't tell you I was going—is that all right?"

"You should tell me, so I don't worry you've got sick."

Other taxi drivers might have preferred to start and stop their cars as instructed, and not taken the risk of rebuff involved in such minute passenger management. I could have rebuffed him—just been the person who paid Isidore to drive, and never found out anything about him and what he knew. He didn't only know the country—its people, its history, food, religions, toilet facilities, and dodgy characters to watch out for—he also spoke better French than I, as well as five Beninois dialects; he knew how to protect me from situations where I might be ripped off, be in physical danger, or simply in danger of making a fool of myself.

*

There were potential dangers in Benin that even Isidore might have found it tricky to extricate me from. Overnight, coup fever might return, blood would spill, and no one would want to marry the white people gadding the streets, because whites about town were usually mercenaries. Benin was a lucrative real-life stomping ground for the *Soldier of Fortune* likes of Bob Denard and was the inspiration for the mercenary-led coup in the novel *The Dogs of War.*

The governmental salsas in and out of communism had led Benin to be nicknamed "The Cuba of West Africa." Many citizens fled. Un-fled young men seemed to have had an allergy to long life and a compulsion to riot in the streets. If this kind of heady atmosphere returned, I could have an untoward Benin experience like Bruce Chatwin's.

In the middle of the interesting old rowdy days, Bruce thought he'd potter around composing a novella. He was assumed to be a mercenary, was roughly arrested and came close to being executed on his way to a hotel swimming pool on a day when peace came apart in a hail of bullets and bazookas. And if such a day came while I was pottering by the same Cotonou hotel pool within firing range of the bullet-scarred presidential palace, I'd be needing Isidore to at least vouch for me as a harmless moron in his care.

Annie Caulfield is a scriptwriter, whose work includes collaborations with the comedian Lenny Henry as well as episodes of This Life. *Her most recent trip to Benin was as adviser and guide to Spice Girl Mel B for her Channel 4 documentary,* Mel B Vodou Princess, *also featuring Isidore the taxi-driver. She has also written* Kingdom of the Film Stars: Journey into Jordan, The Winner's Enclosure, *and* Show Me the Magic: Travels Round Benin in a Taxi, *from which this story was taken.*

* ✱ *

When You Gotta Go

What's that on your shoes?

IN YUCATÁN, WE BOARDED A NICE PUBLIC BUS HEADING for the pyramids at Cobá. This vacation was my great escape from life as a rental property manager. I sat down beside my friend Linda, opposite a dignified Mayan grandma in an immaculate white traditional dress, then realized I had to go. I left my seat and asked the driver in Spanish. "Do I have time for the bathroom?"

"Three minutes."

I ran through the crowded waiting room and into the tile zone. The toilets were a disaster. And none had seats. "I'll try that trick I learned in India," I thought. You stand on the rim and squat. Confident, I loosened my shorts. This bold adventurer could handle filth, easy.

I stepped up with my right foot, then my left.

Over blaring Mexican rock music, I heard a deep groan. The world shifted as a major earthquake shook the planet. Minor panic. My feet slid sideways. Mid-sized panic. The toilet ripped from the tile floor. Leap aside, major panic.

I fell against the locked stall door, pants still down. The bowl crashed over on its side. A wave of icy slime swept through my sandals and right into the warm places between my toes. I lifted my feet in a jig, befuddled as a dog in a dance hall.

Two rusted bolts stood like tiny guards beside the dark sewer hole in the floor. The toilet bowl lay on its side near them, an extinct albino mammoth fallen to its death. It appeared that no one had bothered with that basic plumber's step—bolting the toilet down.

I was sure the station manager would appear in moments, furious. The scene played out as I pulled up my shorts. He'd screech at me, "How did you manage to destroy my toilet?"

Meekly I'd whimper, "I, uh, just...stood on the seat."

"Gringa idiot. Have you people no culture? Do your mothers teach you nothing?"

Next, the police would arrive for the interrogation. They haul me off. I'm thrown to the floor of a courtroom. They impose a hefty fine, plus jail time for attempted terrorism and betrayal of the entire Mexican nation.

Back to reality. Linda had my money, my ID, everything. The bus was leaving at any moment. I still had to go. I slid the bolt and peeked out. Nobody there. The band played on. I slipped into another stall and did my business, air-butt style.

If they came now, being one stall removed from disaster I could claim I knew nothing. "What toilet? What smell?"

Standing in a spreading pool in front of a sink, I washed my hands—no time for the feet. Better get that bus.

I raced past the waiting people, sandals slapping, and climbed the bus steps. "Sorry," I said. The driver shook his head, annoyed at the delay. My sandals squished down the aisle. I sat by Linda, barely able to contain myself as I told her what happened. Laughter erupted through my nose.

The Mayan woman in white kept peering over at me, a look of dismay on her face. What was she thinking? That made me laugh again. The bus started up. She glanced at me once more, this time wrinkling her nose. I sniffed my hands—soap. I smelled the seat back, behind me—hair oil. I sniffed the hair of the man in front of me—shampoo. But there was a hint of something foul in the air.

What was I thinking? It had to be my feet. I poured out half my water bottle on them while she watched. I could see she wanted to ask me something.

Soon, Linda fell asleep. But I could not stop grinning. This near disaster struck me as oddly funny, and I was not sure why. Then it hit me.

I'd got off without getting caught. I didn't have to explain my potty technique. I didn't have to find someone to clean up the mess. Maybe my feet smelled but I didn't have to call the plumber. I didn't have to inspect the mess and figure out who was going to repair the floor or the ceiling below. For a property manager on vacation, the relief bordered on childish glee.

The more I chuckled, the more that Mayan grandma kept checking on me, as if I might actually be a dangerous lunatic.

Barbara H. Shaw thinks she's got it made. She manages properties, writes, edits, teaches, and digs in her garden of earthly delights in Eugene, Oregon. Long a world traveler, every few months she grabs a willing buddy and breaks away to continue exploring the planet. Sounds smug and simple, right? But something wacky always happens.

✦ ✱ ✦

Waiting for the Big "O"

What a difference a letter makes.

A WHITE SANDY BEACH SHIMMERS THROUGH A SMALL CLEAR-ing, and waves relentlessly caress the shoreline. We are on an is-land in the West Indies. We are on our honeymoon. And we've been fighting all week. We have battled in restaurants. We have bickered on the beach. We have brawled in the waves. Strangers hear us coming and going. Strangers want to remain strangers. We are sitting in a rented car on the side of a dirt road almost hidden by overgrown foliage. I am so mad. It is at least ninety degrees outside, but you can see the steam coming out of my ears, and seeping out of the car. If this were a cartoon, there would be horns growing out the roof of our car and a devil's tail would be coming out of the exhaust pipe. The car would be rocking with body parts being thrown from the car windows.

Unfortunately, to make the week just perfect, our rental car is the lemon of all rental cars. The air conditioning doesn't work. The radio is disconnected. There is gum stuck on the driver's side of the windshield and a spring coming out of the passenger seat, right under my behind.

When we pointed this out to the rental agent, he said, with a thick accent, "Hey, maan, it be all we got."

And "Hey, maan, it be all we got," is all we've heard all week.

Orange juice with breakfast? "Papaya today. Hey, maan, it be all we got."

Hot water in the shower? "Cold showers. Hey, maan, it be all we got."

This has not been a good week.

Of the three pieces of luggage we put on board the airplane, two came off. The one we can't find has my asthma medicine and my brand new expensive bathing suit in it. It took me a month to find that bathing suit, to find one that fit just right and was so comfortable and sexy. The lost piece of luggage also has my husband's Tums. My asthma medicine is secondary. My new bathing suit doesn't matter. My husband's Tums? He's a basket case!

"What am I going to do without Tums?" he frets.

I stare at him, wheezing, desperately trying to fill my lungs with air, hoping I can find an island pharmacist who will make a long distance call to my pulmonary specialist. I say, without a hint of nastiness, "Maybe you should lay off the spicy food this week."

To which my husband agonizes, "I won't make it without Tums!"

> I love being married. It's so great to find that one special person you want to annoy for the rest of your life.
>
> ◆
>
> —Rita Rudner

To which I reply in oxygen-poor gasps, tugging at my bathing suit that I had to buy from the store in the lobby, even though it is too small, "I guess you'll have to live with heartburn, honey."

Now we're sitting in the rented car, on the side of a dirt road. I am tugging at my too-small bathing suit. I am wheezing. My husband has heartburn. We haven't had a good cup of coffee in a week. And we are both pissed. We are pissed at the car. We are pissed at the hotel. And we are really pissed at each other.

My husband gets up this morning and says, "Let's fix this vacation now."

I nod my head, somewhat skeptically, but I agree. We need a quick fix for this honeymoon in hell.

My husband goes to the lobby to talk to the concierge. He comes back an hour later and he's bubbling. He's found a perfect place for us to go. He's waving a hand-drawn map. He says it's going to be great.

I'm already upset. Nothing on this island could possibly bring this level of excitement.

Then he starts, "The concierge says it's called Orient Beach. It's on the other side of the island. It will take about an hour to get there. It's a nude beach." My husband's rambling now. "All the movie stars go there. Very private."

"A nude beach?" I ask. "Why'd he tell you about it?"

"Well, we got to talking about surfing, and then he told me. And he said there were great waves."

Surfing. Great waves. I should have read the scribbling in the sand dune.

"Great waves," the concierge says to the boy who spent the summer of his freshman year in high school painting his mother's house to earn money to buy his first long board. "Great waves," he says to the teen who hid surfing magazines under the mattress, to look at the waves, not the girls in the string bikinis. "Great waves," he says to the college student who memorized *Endless Summer*. "Great waves," he says to the young adult who watched surfing specials on television instead of watching the Super Bowl. "Great waves," he says to the homeowner who wanted to decorate our living room around a poster called *Sunset at Doheny*. "Great waves," he says to the man I married who I have never seen on a surfboard.

My husband tells me "nude beach" and "movie stars," expecting me to react with, "Wow, what a wonderful, fabulous, original idea you have," and all he gets is a nasty look from me.

Being the wonderful sport that I am, and wanting to try to salvage this semi-miserable honeymoon in paradise, I decide to go along with it. We grab towels and sun block. My husband hands me the map, and we're on our way to a beautiful nude beach where movie stars hang out, which just by coincidence has great waves.

We drive for an hour. The island is very green, very lush, and extremely humid. It is early when we leave. For miles we drive never seeing another vehicle. We pass many other beaches. The sand is white. The water rushing to the shore comes in long, lingering pushes against the sand. I imagine myself lying in the sand at the water's edge. There are no people on these beaches.

We are, for the first time this week, chatting peacefully. We are even laughing. My husband doesn't have heartburn and I am not wheezing. With some distance between the hotel room and us, this vacation is starting to look more memorable. I'm starting to think that maybe, for once, my husband has had a good idea that won't turn into the Nightmare in the Caribbean.

Then I see the sign.

Orient Beach.

The sign is large. It is brightly colored.

Orient Beach.

Our day is about to be an adventure in paradise. "I got you here," I announce, crumbling the hand-written map and throwing it in the back seat.

My husband looks around. He looks at the sign. "This isn't Orient Beach," he says.

"Yes, it is," I answer, pointing to the sign, "Orient Beach."

"Nope," he says. "This is Rient Beach. We want Orient Beach."

"It is Orient Beach," I continue, not having a clue what he is trying to say.

"Rient Beach," he argues.

Now there's an explanation here, an artistic interpretation. Imagine the word "Rient." From the top of the "R" start an "O." Bring it up and around the back of the "R" so that it looks like a giant "O" going around the word "Rient." It is very clear to me. I can't see the confusion.

I get out of the car.

"Get back in the car! This isn't Orient Beach," he says. He leans over the back of the seat and retrieves the map I just crumbled. "Why did you crumble this?" he mumbles. "I'll get us there."

"We are there," I say. "Look at me." He looks up.

As if my arm is a giant, thick, bold, black magic marker I am dramatizing the big "O" with my arm. I am drawing a giant "O" in the air. "See O——rient. ORIENT. See it? Don't you see the "O"? Come on, think outside the box." I am standing there drawing this giant "O" over and over again in the air for my husband's benefit.

"Get back in the car," he says.

I go up to the billboard. I point to the "O" and draw a giant circle one more time.

"Get back in the car," he says.

I go back to the car. I am standing next to his window. "Think of a giant 'O.' Now put the word 'range' in it. What have you got?"

Expecting to hear, "Orange," all I get is, "Get in the car."

"Orange," I say. "Think, 'O' plus 'range' is orange."

He says nothing.

I try again, "Imagine the word 'liver' with a giant 'O' around it?"

"In the car," he says louder.

I get louder, not liking the bossy tone he's delivering, "Oliver. Think: 'O' plus 'liver' is Oliver!"

I push myself up on the hood, blocking the driver's view. I am visibly enraged. With my finger, I write on the filthy windshield, "vulate." Then I add the giant "O." I am screaming. "Think. 'O' plus 'vulate' is ovulate."

He has stopped talking.

" 'rgasm.' 'O' plus 'rgasm,' Think!" I am writing "orgasm" across the windshield.

Screaming, "verload." I yell and write. "'O' plus 'verload,' OVERLOAD." I am now screaming over the engine. If anyone is hiding in the bushes, they've all jumped into the sea in fear of the mad woman on top of the hood of the car giving a spelling lesson to a baboon who can drive.

I get down from the hood. I open the car door get in, glaring at him, "You are such an AF!" I say.

"You mean ASS?" he says, trying to correct me.

"No," I say. "You are an AF! 'A' 'F' AF."

"What is an AF?" he asks.

"Sam, 'AF' with a big 'O' going around it. YOU ARE AN AF!" I say.

I turn my body away from him and stare out the window, trying to get a view of the great waves before we leave Rient Beach.

And then he shuts off the ignition.

"Oaf," he says. "I am an oaf," he says. He meekly smiles, staring through the windshield with the words "orgasm" and "ovulate" and "overload" written in the filth.

I don't say anything. We both silently get out of the car, grabbing our share of gear from the trunk and head toward the beach, and I swear, as we pass the "Orient Beach" sign, my husband says, "Ya know, that's a really cool logo."

Felice Prager is a professional freelance writer from Scottsdale, Arizona. She also works as an educational therapist with children and adults with learning disabilities. Her work has been published locally, nationally, and internationally, as well as in several anthologies and many Internet sites. More of her humorous stories can be found at Write Funny! (www.writefunny.com). She has not returned to St. Martin since her honeymoon twenty-something years ago, and her husband is still searching for great waves, even though she still has never seen him on a surfboard.

* * *

Emboldened by Women in High Heels

The masses revolt against the petty tyrants.

I DIDN'T WANT TO GO TO THE GREAT WALL. IN BEIJING, I HAD contracted the Mongolian Revenge and had spent the previous two days dashing from bed to bathroom, in a wildly fevered state. I had come to appreciate that the Beijing Palace Hotel has lovely bathrooms with peach-red marble, and plenty of toilet paper. I had also staggered downstairs and found a front desk assistant who was a French intern in-training. She hoped to represent Guerlain cosmetics at a later date, in China. For now, she perfected her Chinese on my behalf, leafing enthusiastically through the dictionary, unable to solve my request. It wasn't until she located the restaurant manager who, with dignity and concern, wrote "broth" in ideograms on a hotel card for me, that I had hope. For breakfast, lunch and supper, all that next week, I pulled out my magic card, something I have saved in my scrap-book, life saver that it was.

The Great Wall is known to many for its t-shirt stands. I already had one claiming: "I climbed the Great Wall," brought back by my parents years ago. But the wall is not known for its toilets. Any of the photos surveying the continuous stretch of wall along the former Mongolian border reveal its remarkable continuity in the *absence* of human comforts. Fortitude, not dependence, is its credo. Still, I thought I might be on the upswing, and when you are going to China or returning, the principal question is, "How about that Great Wall?" The ancient Chinese proverb in my guidebook warned: "One who fails to reach the Great Wall is no hero." So I climbed onto the tour bus at 6 A.M., loaded on Imodium.

I was traveling with an American tour group, which presented its own challenge. We had been to Taiwan and Hong Kong and were now in Beijing. Next we would travel to Nanjing, Xi'an, and Shanghai. We were a group of disparate needs, gestures, and attitudes, twenty professionals tossed together by our dreams of the Orient. We were a mixed salad, and a bad choice put together. For one, the group's stalwart leaders seemed to hate us. Though they were assigned to guide us through thick and thin into the amazing adventure of cultural difference, you could tell they would push you off a bridge if you leaned over in wonder.

Our female leader was revisiting her own Mexican ancestry. Though she was clearly in the wrong location, she sought to circumvent this horrible mistake by refusing to speak English. I am not a language purist—I, too, was raised with the privilege and disconnect of growing up bilingual—but this person works for my same employer in English.

When I asked if a doctor could be summoned to review my high fever and deleterious body fluid loss, this leader deflected my urgent request, demanding imperiously whether I knew that a Latino member of our group was also sick. Was I concerned for her? The next day, when I went to console my fellow sufferer she said she wasn't sick at all. I don't speak Spanish, though, so perhaps she lost her troubles in translation.

Our other leader practiced the ancient Zen Art of Absolute Indifference. Standing aloof from our group, say at the entrance to the Beijing's Summer Palace, he moved only to zoom in like a falcon, replicating a sport once beloved by the Han Dynasty and its royal court, of taloning smaller animals into submission. For instance, when I whispered to someone next to me, "What date did the guide say Emperess Cixi imprisoned Emperor Guangxu?" a sharp talon stabbed my shoulder bone, "The rest of us can't hear when you're talking." When a woman was three minutes late for the tour bus leaving the Forbidden City, he pecked out, "We've all paid for this, we're all waiting. You have no right to hold all of us up." He gained fleeting joy watching her slouch into her seat, publicly humiliated. Still, only the women in the group got reprimanded. It *would* have been helpful to predict which leader was going to appear: The Zen Master of Absolute Indifference or The Falcon Who Attacks Women.

One time, later in the trip, when nearly all had filled the bus and settled in on time as we were eager to greet the air conditioned relief that so contrasted with the July heat we had absorbed walking around Nanjing's massive palace walls and walks, the bus did not move, and we sat and sat and sat. Until one of the middle seats near a large vent began billowing thick, noxious smoke. I had never before considered how fast smoke fills an enclosed space. Billowing is the right word. Someone began screaming, "Fire! Fire!" and in a spastic rush we hopped, leapt, and desperately clambered out. Outside, our one leader gesticulated in Spanish, while the Falcon leader zoomed in on the three agitated women who had been closest to the source of fire, "This is exactly what happens when people arrive late."

"But we weren't late!" they protested.

"The bus was waiting, with its air conditioning on, and it's very hot outside. If the bus sits for too long, the apparatus explodes and catches fire."

"Why didn't you tell us that before?"

"Ah," he said, transforming into the One Who Displays Absolute Indifference, "because *that is not my role.*"

But we were all adults, right? Who needs leaders? I, for one, was mainly concerned with the toilet strategies necessary for The Great Wall. On this June day, I hoped to return without embarrassment.

To be fair, our Zen Master of Misanthropy chose the excellent, less-touristed Jinshanling section of the Great Wall, a two-hour drive from Beijing. It is true that our weaknesses are also our strengths, and his decision made for an astonishing experience. The Great Wall at Badaling can be a Tower of Babel, tour guides shouting in various lan-

——— ☾ ———

Truth be told, I was looking for this adventure-of-a-lifetime to well, sort of, basically change my life. I know it's a lot to ask, but I was shelling out $3,000-plus and figured, lost among the sales verbiage or fine print, there was something to that effect—a promise of personal salvation, clarity of vision, great sex, something. I mean, come on, how can an exotic, physically-challenging trip halfway across the world not realign the stars or transmute my DNA or deliver me from evil? How could it not?

◆

—Laurie Frankel,
"Kili Me Softly"

guages, t-shirts flying from inter-crossing vendor lines, hordes of people steam-rolling through. Not Jinshanling.

It had been raining for three days in Beijing and the sky remained overcast. We were dressed in layers, ready for a range of conditions. Our poised guide had prepared us: "They say in the mountains, the weather is like a child's face, very unpredictable." We bumped along, watching the landscape turn hilly, relishing the deep shades of green the weather wrought, lost in thought, which brought to my mind my other problem.

Like a high school girl who simply cannot stop herself, I had started hanging with the wrong crowd, a good girl pulled into a bad circle. Every day I promised to extricate myself, but these folks were magnetic. They slinked off and talked about what they *saw*. When our guide in Taiwan showed us an intact bronze *ding* tripod, we veered off to look at an intricately carved ceramic *fang zun* (at which point we were exclaiming: *this was made 9,000 years Before Christ, that's 11,000 years ago!!* losing ourselves to the mystery of human talent and inventiveness) and we missed the proper selection of archaeological discoveries, fully annoying our long-suffering leaders. My bad influences included a linguist, a historian, and a poet, the latter who might have been the real root of the problem, as he frequently wondered: "How can I make a poem of this? How?"

Because the Falcon had already targeted us as trouble, I planned to find safer companions at the Great Wall. I sat alone on the bus.

Suddenly our group became focused and alert as the small white van in front of us started littering inordinately. "Ah! They're heading to a funeral," our guide explained, "It's paper money. They throw it so the devil won't follow them." These plastered themselves onto our bus. They were "Hell Bank

Notes," the kind you can buy at Taoist temples to bribe the gods, which flew around us tantalizing in happy swirls. Unfortunately, they did not redeem us to prevent what came next.

We veered off into a narrow old road, curving along a dry riverbed as it climbed farther and farther up toward pine trees. At the half-way point, we found the road was under repair. Piles of rock and dirt interrupted by deep craters tightened our road into a one-lane alley. Still, our driver rounded corners speedily, until all of a sudden we nearly collided with a royal blue work truck. The dance began: which vehicle would back up? Our enormous bus? The boulder-filled truck? Dipping toward the ravine? Crushed against the rugged stone wall? The first time, we backed up, inch by inch by inch. Many from our group fled the front of the bus; others began yelling untranslatable suggestions to our superb Chinese driver. We engaged in this drama, again and again, always inches from disaster, pressing forward, inching back, as if in a nightmare of recurring blue demons.

But we did make it. We arrived at a wide parking lot, the only bus, and we descended. We agreed to find a toilet immediately which thrilled me. In the meantime, the air had lifted. Moist drizzle had become a white mist wafting through the parking lot, the air cool and bright. We were at Jinshanling, ready to greet this UNESCO World Heritage Site, to walk this wall built 2,500 years and many dynasties ago. We learned that the Great Wall stretches for over 50,000 kilometers, across seventeen provinces. Most sections one traverses today were probably built during the Ming Dynasty, but that doesn't make it less impressive. Extending from the Shanhai Pass on the east coast to Jiayu pass in the Gobi desert in the west, it is said to be the only man-made feature visible on earth from the moon.

Because there were no tourists but us, vendors, in a one-to-one ratio now appeared from nowhere, and each targeted a specific individual from our group, walking and talking non-stop, shoving books and replicas at chin level. We hurried up a rugged stairway, surrounded by the swarm of vendors. My blond hair, which always seemed to promise the most foreignness, thus the greatest likelihood of a sale, did not go unnoticed, though that promise was as false as the color. It would be no less than an hour later that I finally bought a Great Wall picture book from the woman who followed me all that time. With her saleswoman's zeal and sheer perseverance, she deserved to be rewarded. Besides, her face was lined and worn, and I had the discomforting awareness that I have so much more in my life than some books to sell. But apparently I overpaid at eight dollars, the rumor flew, and every other vendor came to point at me, exemplar, to convince others of the rightness of an excessive price.

From the mess of steps and twists and vendors, we stepped up onto the ramparts of the Great Wall, astonished to find former Mongolia, ranging mountain crest after mountain crest as far as the eye could see. A sun-burned, brilliant white mist danced between mountains, drawing out their soft outlines in gray and sage and faded green. In the middle of these, like an arrow on a trajectory, the Great Wall at Jinshanling pierced the landscape. It dipped, rose into crenellated ramparts and towers, then tossed itself downhill, to rise next along a mountain crest like a phoenix. I had come here to justify my "I climbed the Great Wall" t-shirt. Instead, I was stunned and unprepared. Wind whistled through the vast landscape, not a soul in sight but us and our vendors.

Our Zen Master Now of Good Ideas had organized an outdoor picnic lunch on the Great Wall. Long foldable tables,

with plastic plates full of rice, dumplings, and skewers of bar-
bequed chicken and pork, awaited us. It didn't matter that I
couldn't eat the food; the place, the moment were enough. In
this dreamy state, I ended up slipping into a chair next to my
troubled old friends. Our leaders told the tour we had one-
and-a-half hours to ourselves before we must be back at
the bus. We could either walk a couple of miles to the cable
station where we would be gondola'd back to the parking lot,
or rest here and make the short descent back.

Half an hour later, my group still sat staring, amazed to
have eaten on the Great Wall, in a silence so fierce it was
beautiful. Then a rush of energy hit us, and we rose, pro-
pelling ourselves forward, our destination: the cable station.
We believed we were young and strong, though we're all
middle-aged and mostly hopeful.

Walking the Great Wall turns out to be no jaunt. The Wall
dips steeply enough to feel like a downhill race. The steps that
follow the inevitable subsequent rise are gigantic, so that you
grasp the step above with your hands as you pull up. I was
told these steps were built for horses to climb, and I believe
it. But we did hike and pause and feel amazed and resume
onward, sweating. During that one hour and half we saw only
one other group, a Scottish family with three sons, bewildered and awe-struck like us. I bless our Zen Master to this
day for his choice, which made the Great Wall what it should
be: astonishing.

Our group philosophized and photographed. At one
tower, we found a cot, and imagined living, sleeping, eating
here, a guard in this vast solitude. "I'd do it in a minute," the
poet claimed. I worried about the toilet issues.

The irony is that we behaved well on this day. We arrived
at the cable station installed modernly to the side of a tower,

sweaty but happy (actually overjoyed) to find a vendor selling cold drinks. No one else was about. We had fifteen minutes to spare to get to the bus on time. My Imodium had worked splendidly. We were golden. We got our cable tickets, smiling at the woman handing them out, and descended about twenty steps to the cable platform. Four women, with up-turned hairdos, in elegant dark and light blue outfits, each in high heels, were huddled against the cable.

We pointed to ourselves, smiling. But they did not smile back. We gesticulated, pointing down hill, indicating our desired destination. But they shook their heads. We began to shout, stupidly, "Us! Down! Now! Go!" But they bowed politely and still shook their heads. I remember losing control and yelling, "Absolutely yes!" They looked chagrined.

Then we saw it, the broken cable. It had taken the previous group down then had broken. I don't know how we pieced this information together. With great concern we were refunded our ticket money. And? We stared at each other, sweat visibly forming on my remaindered group. In a normal situation, it would have been no more than an issue of distance and time, and perhaps a little exhaustion, but our stalwart leaders had made the return time clear. We had a two-and-a-half-hour trip back to Beijing. I remembered being the audience to our Mexican leader one previous time, when she stood at the front of the bus, like Mussolini on his balcony arms raised in a wide V, ordering the bus to "drive off and leave" the stragglers. This she said in English.

We all started shouting again, which did nothing. Which didn't stop us from shouting more. Suddenly one of the elegant women, placed her compact purse under her arm, and gestured to us to follow her. The others nodded. In their spotless apparel, they sinuously curved out the way to a small path veering steeply from the Great Wall. Though the dirt path was nearly vertical for much of its descent, we were emboldened by these women in high heels to take our chances and plunge. They hurried and kept their poise all at once. Those of us on Imodium didn't exhibit the same grace, bolting nervously, clutching our innards.

But we made it. We descended the path where no fee-paying, vendor-enticing tourist goes, guided by cable maidens. We arrived late, of course, but our leaders thought someone had broken a leg, and our cable story unfolded, so we were welcomed, sort of, back onto the bus. "We were going to open your bags and take everything you left," one friendly member spat out. "Yeah, you're lucky we didn't take off." But for us, victory was clear: we climbed the Great Wall just when the cable car broke. We were lost and found. Amazed and bemused. There's something unbeatable about coming in last.

Anne Calcagno has written travel pieces for The New York Times *and the* Chicago Tribune, *and is the editor of* Travelers' Tales Italy.

* ✱ *

Eat My Shorts...If You Can Find Them

One good trick deserves another.

WHOEVER SAID HAWAII WAS PARADISE APPARENTLY NEVER caught a glimpse of a naked obese vacationer. I was called to this self-named God's Country on a business trip, which is one of the many perks of being a writer. My travel companion at the time was a business contact who moonlighted as an unrelenting practical joker. I assumed this personality defect was directly related to a lackluster booty call record. Until this trip, I was never found at the anus end of one of his brainless schemes. After the trip, I ensured that I will never again be. This trip taught my colleague a valuable lesson. Hell hath no clothing when a woman's humiliated.

During the first night in Hawaii, I committed the crime that would cause my humiliation in the proverbial public stocks. I was with my colleague, and we were talking about "adult entertainment" (apparently, sexual harassment laws are void when margaritas and black sand are involved). My misdemeanor occurred when the following words spewed out of my mouth.

"I could never purchase anything from an adult entertainment store. I would be too embarrassed."

I woke up the next morning to a knock on my hotel room door. This surprised me, as I wasn't expecting someone so early. I opened the door to the epitome of "tall, dark, and handsome" who was holding a large cake box with the words "SEXY SWEETS" on it.

"These came for you," he said, obviously trying to repress a smile.

I was a little confused as to what was so amusing about a cake box, but at ten in the morning I'm fairly incapable of speaking in complete sentences, much less coming up with a sarcastic comment. I tipped him and closed the door, wondering who sent me the treats. My secret gift-bearer became apparent when I opened the box. Inside were 6 pastries, each shaped like rather aroused male organs. I was so startled that I actually dropped the box, shattering the perfectly cut Gray's Anatomy pastry models. My eyes turned red from rage, but almost immediately my fire ceased. Sure, it was embarrassing, but it was over. I wasn't going to let him get to me.

Knock. Knock.

Through the peephole I saw the naked inflatable cowboy. Reluctantly, I opened the door. Behind the cowboy was a delivery boy who apparently had hobbits in his gene pool. Aside from the cowboy pool toy, he was also carrying a two-foot-tall Christmas tree exclusively decorated with condoms and anal beads. By this time, several hotel guests were passing by and snickering on the way to their rooms. I snatched my cowboy toy and my Condom Tree, shoved some bills in the delivery man's hands, and closed the door, praying for the ordeal to be over.

Unfortunately, not only is my colleague an unrelenting

practical joker, he is also a fairly wealthy one who can devote large sums of money to his gaggery. Within the next half hour, my door was knocked on approximately seven times, and I received a potpourri of everything that could possibly vibrate, bind, and spank, as well as several sets of stocks, and a trio of obese men in G-strings prepared for a strip-o-gram. By the end, my hotel room was fully furnished with a multitude of edible panties, whips, chains, prophylactics, and flavored whipped creams. The last knock was the most mortifying. Apparently, through my ordeal, I forgot to put the "Do Not Disturb" sign on the door, and I threw open the door to the maid. She took one look inside my Dr. Ruth's Vacation Home, and fainted. I called the hotel manager, and explained to him the situation. After about fifteen minutes, he was able to stop laughing. As if by clockwork, my colleague called.

"You're toast," I said.

"In your dreams," he laughed.

His laughter was relatively short-lived.

Interestingly, it was God who came up with the comeback. That afternoon, my colleague and I were seated on the beach, and he was still giving me a hard time about my "special deliveries." I took it all in stride, as I knew I was going to get my revenge. However, I couldn't know it would come so soon.

At that point, he decided to take a swim. In all honesty, I was happy to get rid of him, so I could engross myself in the latest Stephen King novel. I cracked open the spine, and hunkered down to my literary adventure.

About two chapters in, I heard my colleague yelling to me. I looked up slightly, not willing to be torn away from my book, when my eyes landed on a familiar set of swim shorts washing up on shore. I looked out to sea, and there was my colleague standing in the middle of the ocean giving me the universal hands-clasped-over-the-crotch "I'm naked in a public place" sign. Apparently, those thirty pounds he lost specifically for this trip were coming back to haunt him. To add to his plight, Hawaiian water is rather transparent. Within minutes, several observers on the beach were pointing at him and laughing, as his hands were doing nothing in the way of covering his nether region.

I walked over to the red shorts and picked them up. I twirled them in my hand for a little while, smiling smugly at him.

"Payback's a bitch!" I yelled.

I could barely hear his pleads, curses, and threats. His eyes followed me as I took his shorts to the nearest palm tree, and using my softball pitching arm, threw them high up in the tree. Island legend said they are currently being used in place of a lighthouse to guide boaters to shore. Then, I gave him a large smile, waved at him, and retreated to the hotel, ignoring the death threats spewing from his mouth.

He made it back to the hotel an hour later, surprisingly without an indecent exposure charge. Apparently, while getting in touch with his Adam and Eve side in the water, he was able to locate two very large shells to cover himself, until a group of older ladies took pity on him and gave him one of their beach towels. As I opened the door, his eyes bore holes in me as if he was Jesus bumping into Judas for the first time in heaven. We declared a truce, and he vowed never to play a practical joke on me ever again.

When we got back to work, nothing of the two practical jokes was mentioned out of respect for my dignity and his intimate tan lines. But from time to time I can't seem to resist leaving a naked Ken doll in his office's aquarium.

Jenn Dlugos is a comedian and comedy writer from New England. She has a column at Just Laugh Magazine *(www.justlaugh.com), and is the author of a book about the humorous end of health care,* Public Health Disturbance. *You can learn more about Jenn at her web site, www.deJENNerate.com.*

* ✱ *

Fruit Bats and Healers

Whoops, damn, ouch, wow!

RICKY ATTACHED HIMSELF TO US ON THE OUTSKIRTS OF Bukkitingi, a Sumatran hill station we'd arrived in the night before. Amped up on the novelty of oatmeal and cool mist after many weeks of tropical heat, I had agreed to join Greg on a brisk constitutional in the surrounding countryside, figuring I'd have loads of time to explore the red-brick town in search of the ideal café in which to fritter away the hours, writing in my journal and consuming high-caloric, cold-weather food. We meandered through valleys and forded a small stream accompanied by a band of five-year-olds who threw dirt clods at us when we refused to give them cigarettes. Ricky, on his way into town, heard our protests and shot-putted the little gangsters away by their ears. "Bad boys," he remarked, shrugging his thin shoulders with the seen-it-all cynicism at which fourteen-year-olds excel. Then he reversed direction to walk with us, filling us in on a few details of his life. He lived nearby with his mother, father, and seven younger siblings and he wasn't in school because he had no money. He seemed like a bright kid, full of questions, including a request for a cigarette. "Marlboro," he nodded, taking two. "Cool." We meandered around for an hour or so, cutting across fields and taking back-country roads. Ricky took us to a cottage belonging to a jewelrymaker where I bought two pairs of dainty silver filigree earrings, figuring I could give them to someone as a present. I didn't want our new friend to go without his tiny commission just because I was the hippie hubcap type. He asked us if we wanted to see the flying foxes. Having bought the earrings and participated in the obligatory bushwhack through nature, I was inclined to head back to the civilized pleasures of Bukkitingi, but Greg was intrigued. Ricky was a bit hard-pressed to describe these miraculous creatures to English-speaking visitors, since, he reminded us, he had no money to attend school. Greg asked him how much he would charge to lead us to their lair, while I asked how far it was, not relishing a long tramp back. I had a hunch that there was slim chance of the flying foxes living up to the image in my head of the North American terrestrial model outfitted with ruddy wings to match its auburn pelt.

After half an hour's farther walk, Ricky led us through a meadow of waist-high weeds still damp with dew. We emerged on the lip of a gorge, a deep chasm choked with bamboo and tangled vegetation. Pulling the checkered sarong he wore like a shawl over his head babushka-style, Ricky indicated a dead tree rising from the gorge floor. It was a gnarled old devil, the kind that throws apples at Dorothy in *The Wizard of Oz,* but several stories taller.

Squinting, I could make out dozens of withered black papayas hanging from its leafless branches, but nothing resembling a winged fox. "Can we get closer?" Greg asked.

"Closer O.K.," Ricky said, picking his way a few feet downhill in his rundown rubber flip flops. Greg and I followed gingerly, choosing our footing carefully on the muddy incline. Suddenly one of the papayas opened up like a Delorean and took to the skies. After a few circles, it returned to the tree, wrapped itself back up in its wings and roosted beneath a branch. Flying foxes, please, these were nothing but big bats. No wonder they were all asleep! Bats are nocturnal creatures. "Flying fucking dogs," Ricky giggled. Pleased with the ring of his deftly deployed slang, he repeated himself at top volume, clapping his hands for good measure. "Flying fucking dogs!"

Pumping their leathery wings, the bats rose from the tree in a great black cloud and I tumbled headfirst into the gorge, dislocating my knee. I came to a rest in a clump of bamboo several yards down, but the pain was so great I wouldn't have cared if I'd bounced all the way to the bottom, dashing my brains out on a jagged rock. I immediately recognized what had happened to me, even before I came to a stop. Ever since my original injury, when a rogue kindergartner darted in front of me while I was running laps in Miss Trotter's high school gym class, my knee had gone out at least once a year, but never so badly as this. Having since delivered two babies without pain medication, I can say now with certainty that the sensation rivals the most wrenching contractions of childbirth. Imagine your leg as a green stick. Now imagine a giant child snapping that stick in half, except the stick, being green, won't break all the way, so the kid twists it in an attempt to pull it apart. Don't forget to invest this image with all the excruciating, slow motion, oh God, I-think-I'm-going-to-throw-up pain you can drum up. I sprawled on my back, my wraparound skirt unwrapped, gasping like a fish in the bottom of a boat. Greg's head floated upside down in the distance. I could just barely hear him calling to me over the deafening storm of my own hyperventilation. Clutching at roots and vines, Greg managed to scramble down to my level, with Ricky skidding somewhat less urgently behind.

"Oh my God, Ayunee, what happened? Are you O.K.?" Wedging his foot securely against the bamboo stand, he knelt in the mud that was fast seeping through my clothing.

"My knee," I wheezed. The sky was white. In other years, my kneecap had popped back into place immediately, leaving me breathless and hurting, but able to hobble unassisted to the nearest source of ice and conciliatory beverages. I'd learned to milk my trick joint, claiming dislocation whenever I wanted to worm out of work at the last minute. The next day, I'd show up strapped into the bulky white cotton leg brace I'd acquired in college, smiling gratefully as co-workers forced me to sit down while they did all of my Xeroxing. What a sham! People with dislocated knees can barely stand, let alone temp, even with a removable brace! I remembered the agony when Miss Trotter had insisted that I pick myself off the floor to "walk it off." The next morning an orthopedist, whose daughter had gone to camp with me, put me in a cast for a month and still it killed, but not as bad as this. Bracing myself for the worst, I unsquinched an eye to assess the damage. My kneecap remained far left of its customary center. If my foot had been pointing in the same direction, I would have achieved perfect balletic turn-out.

"O.K., let's get you out of here." Greg slid his arms around me to hoist me into a sitting position, which given the extremely slick conditions, was a task akin to retrieving a greased watermelon from the deep end of the pool.

"Stop! That hurts," I yelped. "Got to catch my breath."

"O.K. O.K." Greg looked a little desperate, kneeling with one arm pinned beneath me. "Do you think you can walk?"

"I don't know. Fix my skirt!"

Ricky smirked as Greg rearranged the fabric to cover my panties. "Maybe scared by flying foxes," Ricky said, seizing my arm and yanking hard.

"No!" I cried, as a deadly electric eel lit up my left leg. "Let me lie here!" We remained there for several minutes while my knee ballooned to grapefruit dimensions.

"What did you do the last time this happened?" Greg asked.

"You mean this bad?" I replied between gritted teeth. "I went to an orthopedist who reset my knee and put me in a cast."

"Did you have to have surgery?"

I shot Greg a look that said he would know all of this if he'd been listening carefully for the two years we'd been together. "No, he stuck a big needle in my knee and drained off all this fluid and then I felt better. I *should* have had surgery the first time, when I was still in school and living at home. *Owww,* this really kills."

"Flying fucking foxes," Ricky chuckled.

We made it back to the guesthouse, a tidy low-slung building on a hill above the main drag. After spending our first night in a grubby hotel on the noisy main drag, we had gone looking for better quarters and found this before embarking on what turned out to be the flying-fox debacle. The new digs made for a pleasant enough sick room, with clean sheets on a comfortable bed situated beneath a window opening onto a small shaded porch. The lady of the house, seeing me limping in, made appropriate noises of *oh you poor thing* and rushed to help make me comfortable. "*Es?*" I asked, pointing to my knee, now swollen to the size of a good-sized cantaloupe. *"Ada es?"*

While Greg was out fetching the doctor, I received a visit from Bapak, Ibu's husband. I didn't know their real names. *Ibu*—mother—and *Bapak*—father—are Indonesian terms of respect, along the lines of ma'am and sir. Our hosts did seem to embody Mom and Dad, living in an apartment behind the guest rooms with their unmarried adult children. Other relatives arrived on motor scooters throughout the day, dropping off grandchildren and picking up pots of delicious-smelling food. I enjoyed the hubbub of their family life. Bapak was clearly the boss, dispatching his handsome, bashful sons on various errands and muttering as Ibu and other women I took to be her sisters laughingly did his bidding. He strutted around the property in a sarong and tank shirt, his comportment that of a grizzled but still strong Boston bull terrier who doesn't see the humor in his self-importance. "Ah," he rasped, glaring at my knee. "Sick. Need massage."

"Oh, that's O.K., thanks, Pak," I said, as cheerful and polite as my friends and I used to be around each others' parents. "My, uh, husband is getting the doctor."

"Doctor, bah." He scowled and kneaded the air. "Massage good!"

> This is the twenty-first century. Forget girl power (*so* nineties)—this is the age of butt-kicking babes, of girls with guns. I'm meant to be able to wrestle bears all on my own—*and* keep my frosted-pink manicure intact.
>
> ◆
>
> —Polly Evans,
> *It's Not About the Tapas*

"Maybe later. Now, just resting."

His square little head bobbed in approval. "O.K., sleep good, too. Then…massage!" He seemed to be waiting for something, so I closed my book and my eyes. Being careful not to disturb the injured knee resting on a pillow, he covered me with a lightweight blanket and padded out, leaving the door ajar. I stayed like that for a couple of minutes, then, feeling like a kid sneaking comics with a flashlight under the covers, I cracked my book back open. Man, that Somerset Maugham! He was something! Imagine traveling around Southeast Asia by freighter, evening clothes packed in your steamer trunk, presenting your letter of introduction to a backwater Dutch government rep, drinking *stengahs* with him on the porch after dinner…. After the third one, the Dutchman confides that his wife murdered her lover in the bush. Bapak banged the door open, rocketing me back into the present. I propped myself up on my elbows, rubbing my eyes as if I'd been sleeping. He sloshed a reddish-brown liquid inside an old peanut butter jar. "*Jamu*," he informed me. "For make well."

"Oh?" I stalled. I remembered reading about *jamu*, the traditional Indonesian folk medicine, in Lonely Planet but I had pictured it more appetizing, like freshly ground pesto, not motor oil mixed in the open sewer. "Do you use *jamu*?"

He gave a virile grunt. "Every day *jamu*." His face clenched as if gripped by a horrible migraine, then unscrewing the lid, he pretended to dip his hand into the foul broth and apply some to his forehead. "*Jamu* no more head hurt." Groaning, he rolled his shoulders back and forth, seeking relief from back pain. "Put *jamu*, make good, strong!" He paraded in a circle, inviting me to admire his healthy, barrel-shaped body. "*Jamu*."

"Can I see?" Bitter mentholated fumes assaulted the delicate membranes of my eyes as he thrust the jar under my nose. Little unidentified bits were floating on the brackish surface.

"Very nice. Maybe later, O.K.?"

"You must massage," he growled, a true believer. He stuck a paw into the *jamu* jar and seized my knee with an eagle's firm grasp. Apparently not one to suffer torture stoically, I let out an involuntary yell that threw us both. Bapak clucked sympathetically, as if reassuring a tearful grandchild. "Ooh, hurt. Hurt a little bit." Again, he sunk his fingers into the swollen fruit of my knee.

I jackknifed forward and grabbed his wrist. "Please! Please, no *jamu*! No massage! Let me sleep!"

Reluctantly, he recapped the *jamu*, rubbing the excess from his palms into the muscles of his neck. He could see that he'd have to proceed slowly with me, even if it meant I'd heal less quickly than someone like him, who bore the initial discomfort in order to get the immediate benefits of that awesome *jamu* power. "I come back. You must massage. Massagggggggggggge." Sniffling a little, I curled into as fetal a position as I could manage.

Greg came back alone. "I found the fancy hotel, but they said they don't have a house doctor."

"What?! Well, did they give you a recommendation at least?"

"No, I think they wanted to get rid of me. It was more of a businessman kind of place, you know? They did give me some ice." He held up a small plastic bag half filled and fast melting.

"Wow, so generous," I groused.

"Yeah, they weren't very happy about it. I got you some Bang-Bangs though," he brightened, lining up two chocolate bars next to a bunch of bananas and a couple of sodas. "What's that weird smell?"

"*Jamu*. The old guy kept trying to massage my knee with it. Do me a favor, if you see him coming with an old jar full of reddish-brown shit, tell him I'm sleeping. He won't take no for an answer."

"So, what do you think we should do about this?" I hoisted my good leg alongside the other, so we could compare. "Jesus, that looks really bad. Is it going to be all right? Do you think maybe if you just stay off it, take it easy for a couple of days, it'll go down on its own?"

"Yeah, probably," I lied hopefully. It was sort of like hoping that finger you accidentally lopped off with the paper cutter will grow back. "If there's no doctor around, I don't see what we've got to lose by waiting around for a day or two. Why rush into things?" Greg suggested that I try to walk a little, so I didn't get too stiff. Whimpering, I inched to the edge of the bed, lowered my legs over the side and burst into tears. We decided to dine in that evening, Greg gallantly, if uncharacteristically, pretending to be satisfied by a repast of candy and bananas, even when the mouthwatering aromas of the family's dinner wafted in through the open window.

The knee appeared no better in the morning, but we rationalized that miracles seldom happen overnight.

It was time for a serious discussion about how to deal with this problem, which showed no signs of improvement. My neck and lower back were developing muscular complaints of their own, from constantly torquing my body into a position most comfortable for my fragile knee. If only this had happened in Jakarta, where Greg's brother lived in an air-conditioned apartment, with a fully stocked refrigerator and dozens of hours of *The Simpsons* on tape! Sam would have known where to go to get my knee treated in a timely, Western fashion. Of course, I would never have slipped down a muddy gorge in Jakarta. Maybe I'd have fallen into a canal choked with sewage, but plenty of people lived in cardboard shanties on the banks, doing their laundry and bathing in it and nothing happened to them, or at least they all didn't die instantly! I was beginning to realize that this type of injury is better handled by an authority figure, my parents, a personal connection in the State Department, even a physician retained to treat the hot flashes and hangovers of luxury hotel guests. Greg and I had no one except ourselves and an old man who thought the best medicine resided in a peanut butter jar. Since Greg was home to prevent any assaults by *jamu*, we were able to leave the door ajar to create some cross ventilation. We were reading in bed when a bright-eyed person with close-cropped hair, gap teeth, and a small heart dangling from the hoop in his ear poked his head into the room. "I hear you're having a bit of trouble here," he said in a thick Australian accent. "Mind if I have a look?" Most girls aren't keen on hearing "that looks nasty, all right" when they display their stems to a new acquaintance of the male persuasion, but in this instance, I was glad to have validation.

We explained the circumstances that had led to the injury and our fruitless search for a Western doctor. "I see. And just what exactly did you have in mind for this doctor to do?" I told him about the father of the girl I had gone to camp with draining off the accumulated fluid the first time it happened. He took a deep drag on his unfiltered cigarette. "Yeah, I don't think you want anyone sticking a needle in your knee in this country." He told us that his name was Geoff and that he'd been here for some months, studying an indigenous martial art with a family who lived in a small village in the mountains. Every Saturday, he rode his motorbike into Bukkitingi to pick up his mail and see a kung-fu movie, spending the night at our guesthouse before returning the next day. "I don't know how you'd feel about this, but I've got a man who fixes me up when my teacher gives me too good a beating. He's not a doctor—more like an Islamic holy man who knows a thing or two about bones—but if you're up for it, I could take my bike and see if he's around. He might be able to help you.

I looked at Greg. "Up to you," he said, raising his eyebrows dubiously.

"O.K., if it's no trouble."

"No trouble," Geoff smiled rakishly, pulling his helmet on. He sped away and we waited. One hour went by. Two.

"Do you think he forgot about you?" Greg asked.

"No, he probably couldn't find the guy. He said he wasn't sure if he'd be around. Maybe it's for the best. It's not necessarily a good idea to let a witch doctor start monkeying around with your bones."

"You said it, not me," Greg testified, heading out to replenish my Bang Bang supply.

Shortly after he left, Geoff's motorbike roared to a stop outside the window. He came in, followed by a bashful older man half his height. "Sorry it took us so long. He had to finish his badminton game," Geoff apologized. He translated my elaborate thanks into Bahasa, while the bonesetter nodded and shook his head, seemingly embarrassed by all the fuss. "He wants to know which knee it is."

"Oh, this one," I said pointing to the left. When I'd heard them coming, I'd made an effort to pull myself together, smoothing my black chiffon skirt down modestly. Very deli-

cately, the bonesetter picked up my hem and started rolling it
up like the most precious spliff on the planet.

"This is an embarrassing thing for him," Geoff whispered.
"He's very devout." I was glad I wasn't wearing my wraparound skirt. When he'd unveiled the swollen eyesore, he
stopped, considering. Using a touch no heavier than a but-
terfly's eyelash, he allowed his fingertips to isolate the area of
injury, then turned to make an inquiry of Geoff. "He says it's
very hot. Does it hurt?"

"I tell her she must massage," Bapak interjected from the
doorway, where he stood with his jar of *jamu* at the ready.

"Well, he's not hurting me if that's what he means. The
main problem is, I can't walk without feeling like someone's
twisting a giant knife around in there. I can't walk at all really."

Geoff translated and the bonesetter made a face that told
me he understood. He tapped the knee lightly, apparently
considering the best course of action, then came around to
the foot of the bed. The crowd of onlookers who had formed
at the window murmured amongst themselves, eager to see
what he would do. To my bafflement, he started playing "This
Little Piggie Went to Market," humming a little as he wiggled
my toes one after another. Wanting to seem companionable,
I giggled a little. He laughed good-naturedly and started over
with the big toe. I glanced at Geoff. He turned his palms up,
shrugging. The bonesetter pulled a little harder, yanking from
the bases where the toes joined the foot. It hurt a little bit to
tell the truth and whatever the joke was, it was wearing thin.
"Oww," I said, still smiling, hoping he'd realize this was a bit
rougher than I liked.

"Oww," he agreed pleasantly, easing up on the pressure. I
laughed to show there were no hard feelings. He hummed his
innocuous little tune. My jaws ached from my good-sport

grin. Without warning, he pounced, pinning my thigh to the mattress as he wrenched my shin like someone throwing the lever on a seldom-used electric chair. The dislocated knee snapped back into alignment with the resounding crack of a gunshot. The audience at the window burst into spontaneous applause while I gasped, trying to regain my composure following an exquisite blast of torture that was over almost before it had begun. "You having a party?" Greg asked, appearing in the doorway with a small sack of Bang Bangs. Beside him, Bapak looked disgruntled, no doubt thinking that his *jamu* would have done the job just as well, had I not interfered with his treatment plan. As far as I was concerned, the bonesetter could have declared himself the great and powerful Oz right there, but as I suspected, he was not a man to milk it. Instead, he gestured that I should take a few steps. Having played the titular role in the Indianapolis Junior Civic Theatre's production of *Heidi,* I could appreciate the drama inherent in the moment. Weak and wary of falling, I still rose to my feet and staggered unassisted to Greg, just like Clara, the lame rich girl whom Heidi's infectious can-do spirit gives the courage to eighty-six that wheelchair! It was quite remarkable. It also made me realize how completely rat screwed we would have been if chance hadn't placed us in the same guesthouse as Geoff.

"How much should I pay him?" I asked.

Geoff said that there was no set figure, but suggested a figure so low by American health care standards, it was practically Canadian. Even when I doubled it, it was still less than the co-pay for seeing an in-network doctor. My miracle worker tucked it into the pocket of his short-sleeved dress shirt with a courteous word of thanks, though the young men pressing against the window screen to get a gander at the wad seemed impressed. I felt like I should have offered to buy him a goat in addition, but before I knew it, he was straddling the motorbike, looking almost wizened behind the tan, tank-shirted Australian. For all I knew, he'd saved me by making a house call on his day off.

Ayun Halliday is the sole staff member of the quarterly zine, The East Village Inky *and the author of* The Big Rumpus: A Mother's Tale from the Trenches *and* No Touch Monkey! And Other Travelers' Lessons Learned Too Late, *from which this story is excerpted. She is* BUST *magazine's Mother Superior columnist and also contributes to NPR,* Hipmama, *and more anthologies than you can shake a stick at without dangling a participle. She lives in Brooklyn, where she's hard at work on her next book,* Job Hopper. *Visit her web site at www.ayunhalliday.com*

★

While visiting Barbados, we ate our breakfast at an outdoor buffet. The maitre'd met us with a smile and a warning not to feed the monkeys. We had only arrived the night before and I hadn't seen any monkeys at all. I thought he was just being charming since the building sat at the edge of the rainforest.

And then I saw: a large wide-eyed monkey sitting at my feet. I was delighted. My husband took one look at the creature and reminded me what the maitre'd had said about not feeding the monkeys. But those sweet little eyes were begging for a handout. I tried to ignore it, but when I felt my skirt being tugged on, I caved in. When no one was looking, I broke off a piece of banana and lowered my hand down to give it to my little friend. He, of course, snatched it out of my hand and ran down the brick stairway and disappeared into the jungle. I thought I was pretty smart having outwitted both the maitre'd *and* my cautious husband. But I was wrong.

On the second morning, the maitre'd was waiting for us and he wasn't smiling. As we were escorted to our table by the steps, I could see three large monkeys just sitting there.

On the third morning when we arrived for breakfast, the maitre'd took us to the same table as before. I could hear them before I saw them...MONKEYS. Not three or six, but forty or fifty noisy, chattering monkeys lined both window sills and were crowded onto the stone steps looking for a handout. I just stood there not knowing what to say or do. A platoon of broom-wielding waiters rushed in to disperse them. Monkeys scattered everywhere!

—Diane Kolb, "Don't Feed the Monkeys"

* * *

The Pen is Mightier Than the Prick

All good girl scouts come prepared.

I WASN'T GOING TO GET MOLESTED ON THE SUBWAY. I'D heard the tales. In Nagoya, Japan, a conservative city where few other foreigners lived, they pack you so tightly into the subway cars that one fellow foreign exchange student swore he'd ridden to the university an inch off the ground. Another had been unable to lift his arms from his sides to cover his mouth when he sneezed.

But those were the male adventures. The women felt strange pressures against their thighs and looked down to find someone jacking off against them—but whose penis was that? Passengers twisted around each other in humiliating, X-rated positions; it was impossible to connect a hand to an arm to a face, let alone a penis to a torso. Another woman had been unable to move her hands from the bar she clung to for balance as fingers slunk up her shirt and dug beneath her bra. "Whose hand?" she shouted in Japanese. "*Dare no te?*"

The best tactic I could take in defense of my twenty-year-old body, I believed, was to make every subway rider afraid of me. If the doors started to close before I'd boarded, I pulled them apart and stepped in like any New Yorker, but in Nagoya they stared as though a gorilla had pounced into their car. I grabbed a rail angrily and gave my neighbors a hard glare. They were polite businessmen, but chances were good a perv stood in one of those suits. With my free hand (which I'd kept raised above my head while boarding in case I couldn't get it up there once the doors had closed) I flipped my vocabulary flashcards. These were held together by a metal ring I wore around my index finger, and I held them high so every black magic-markered word screamed in plain view: *Pervert!…Molester!…Castrate!*

I got space. The businessmen against me already balanced on other people's feet, but they found they could settle another few inches away. I enjoyed luxurious rides.

Then one day, while walking from class toward the subway down a narrow, nearly vacant street, a man who looked not much older than me asked for directions. Anyone who's ever met up with a flasher, exhibitionist, or what-sexual-dysfunction-have-you knows that when a man asks a lone female for directions, warning sirens should go off in her head. But it was one of the first warm April days, and the new spring had summoned in me a feeling of goodwill and swollen my sense of invulnerability—I was, after all, the only American female I knew in Japan to evade all perverts for the past eight months, and I felt particularly clever for it. So instead of pausing to wonder why a Japanese man might ask a foreigner for directions, I noticed how clean and spring-like he appeared in his white pants and white button-down shirt.

"Yes, the university is that way," I was saying. "No, just up there." The man pointed everywhere, at the houses lining the street and the shreds of clouds in the sky. But he was only pointing with one hand. When I looked down to see what the other might be doing, he grabbed me and pulled me against him.

"Please, touch it," he said. "Please." He held out his monstrosity and lurched toward my hand.

I pushed him away and stepped back. But I didn't leave. How dare he ruin my eight-month-long pervert-free record—and here, in such an easy, obvious, vacant street? I wasn't even on the subway, the most challenging terrain for a pale blonde. I wanted revenge.

I could take him, I thought. He was my height but skinnier, and I'd had no trouble pushing him off me.

The man mistook my assessment of him as a sign that I was thinking over his request and he begged profusely. "I will be so grateful," he said and groaned.

I dropped my backpack and quickly rummaged through it searching for something I could use as a weapon. In the distance behind him two women turned onto the street, so if all else failed, other people were around now to help. I thumbed past books and notebooks and crumpled papers—why didn't I carry a knife or mace or a spiked bat?

In the end I pulled out my pen and uncapped it. A blue ballpoint. At the very least, I could scrawl all over his white spring clothes. Holding it like a spear, I charged.

He tore down the street and I chased after him. Couldn't I gouge his eyes out with my pen, or put a puncture hole in his cock? But he was far too fast for me as he raced for his life, still holding himself with one hand.

Lara Ephron, an editor, recently took an extended honeymoon traveling with her husband through Europe and central Turkey, where she explored astonishing phallic rock formations in a fairy-tale setting and returned home pregnant. She lives in Portland, Oregon, with her husband, dog, and big belly.

* ✳ *

Blind Faith

God's work is never done.

By THE TIME WE ARRIVED IN MONACO I DIDN'T WANT TO hear anymore about The Lord. I'd had enough of traveling with Trudy. One year earlier, when I first met her at a local hiking group, a summer-long trip through Europe seemed like a good idea. We were both just out of college with a desire to travel and a need to test our recent financial and social independence. What I didn't discover until we'd landed at Heathrow Airport was that somewhere between agreeing on which countries to visit and packing our bags, Trudy had become a born-again Christian.

"Praise the Lord," she announced when we got off the plane, and again when both our backpacks appeared on the baggage carousel, and again, when we found a ride into London. Throughout England and France, Trudy praised God for almost everything we did, saw, and ate. I could tell she was caught up in the excitement of her newfound spirituality, and had she kept her enthusiasm to the frequent but brief exaltations to "Praise the Lord," or as she sometimes preferred,

"PTL," our friendship might not have been strained to the breaking point.

Faith, for me, was a private matter. But for Trudy, it was something to celebrate and share. No London shopkeeper we met was left without a biblical quote to ponder. No French baguette or wedge of fromâge was consumed without Trudy's reverent thanks. She glowed with the excitement and self-assurance of the recently converted while I winced with embarrassment and, increasingly, irritation.

After two weeks of togetherness, we were both ready to spend time apart. We split up at Monaco's seaside. I lay in the sun with a romance novel in my hands and my bathing suit top in my daypack. Trudy sat in the shade with the Bible in her lap and The Lord Jesus Christ in her heart. Four hours later I felt ready to share the same country with my travel mate again. Slipping t-shirt and shorts over my swimsuit, I set off to find her.

"Oh God," I sighed when I caught sight of Trudy. Standing next to her was a man holding her Bible. Neatly tucked into the rolled-up sleeve of his white cotton t-shirt was a pack of Marlboro's.

"This is Andre," she gushed. "He wants to learn about The Lord."

"Yes, Trudy is teaching me." Andre spoke with an accent I couldn't place. A thin black curl escaped from his slicked-back hair. The errant strand fell across his angular cheek, encircling a fat mole on his otherwise smooth, olive skin. His dark eyes were too busy staring at Trudy's slender figure to meet mine. Andre's interest in her, I was sure, had nothing to do with embracing The Lord.

My plan to clue Trudy in was delayed by her sudden invitation to Andre to join us at a nearby outdoor café. The garden courtyard was nearly empty. Andre wound his way to a table beneath a gnarled tree. He reversed his chair and coiled himself around the backrest, then beckoned Trudy to sit in the chair next to him. "Tell your friend to get the waiter," he commanded.

I laughed, certain Andre's rude behavior would repel Trudy and we would be done with him. But she just grinned and moved her chair out of the sun. Andre squeezed a cigarette from his sleeve. He leaned in toward Trudy, dismissing my presence. Acrid smoke slithered up between them. I sat down and stared at Trudy, willing her to see the snake beside her.

Trudy filled the silence by quoting scripture until the waiter arrived with our ice cream and lemonade. She babbled on about her desire to speak in tongues while I shoveled vanilla ice cream into my mouth. Andre must have misunderstood the point of Trudy's story or become overexcited hearing the words "desire" and "tongues" in the same sentence. "You have sex with me," he interrupted. I looked up from my dessert, then blinked. Andre was staring at me.

I turned to Trudy, thinking, Can you believe this guy? But Trudy glared back at me as if I had purposely lured her innocent convert from Jesus.

"No, Andre," I said, emphasizing each word for both his sake and Trudy's, "I am not having sex with you."

"You are not my friend," he hissed. "You are stupid and a child." He took a drag from his cigarette. "Trudy is a woman."

"Yeah, well, 'the woman' and I are going now." I stood up and threw my daypack over my shoulder. "By ourselves."

Andre stood up, too, sending his chair clattering against the cobblestone. He leaned across the table. "Trudy is coming with me."

"What? No she's not." I tried to catch the eye of one of the other customers, but no one seemed to notice our mini-drama playing out at the back of the café.

"She's going with me to my hotel." Andre's voice was both matter-of-fact and forceful. "I bought her a drink at the beach." Trudy's mouth hung open. The accusation previously seared on her face crumbled into disbelief.

"Tell him, Trudy. Tell him you're not going with him." Trudy continued to gape in silence. "She's not going with you," I answered for her, meeting Andre's gaze. "She didn't understand what you wanted when you bought her the drink. Tell him, Trudy." Lot's wife showed more reaction when she turned into a pillar of salt. I grabbed Trudy's bag from the table and shoved it in her lap. "We're leaving."

Disgusted, I walked away not caring whether Trudy followed or not.

Moments later, I saw her crossing the street towards me. Her sunscreen and shade-pampered face appeared whiter than usual. Hallelujah, she's seen the light, I thought, stopping by the harbor so she could catch up. She's going to realize how blinded she's been and become the Trudy I'd first met. We might never share the same religious beliefs, but I had faith in the friendship we built over the past year. My frustration and anger melted. I leaned against the wall overlooking the water and waited for the return of my friend—the friend who laughed at bawdy jokes and talked of French pastries and famous museums without invoking Jesus's name every third sentence.

"I thought," Trudy said breathlessly when she caught up with me, "I thought he wanted to learn about The Lord."

I closed my eyes, pressing them with the palms of my

hands until they hurt. Her confession was so much less than I'd hoped for. But it was a start.

This was going to be a long summer. Praise The Lord.

Susan Lyn McCombs, who was reborn ten years ago as a writer, has had the good fortune to travel with companions holding a diversity of interests and passions. She is a contributing writer and editor to the Best Places guidebook series. Her articles and stories appear in news-papers, magazines, and in the Travelers' Tales anthology, Family Travel.

* ✱ *

The Barf Boat

The road to paradise is paved with—well, let's not get into that.

CAPE VERDE ON LAND IS EVERYTHING THE POETS PROMISE. Cape Verde at sea, aboard the Ribeira Ferry, is where the poetry ends in an abrupt splat.

A former Portuguese colony off the West African coast, Cape Verde's ten islands have a romantic, Mediterranean feel. The streets are cobbled, edged by buildings in faded shades like pistachio, coral, sandy yellow, and sea blue. Fishing boats bob in the bay, surrounded by jagged mountains. Outdoor cafes are filled with smiling people sipping espresso, *ponch* (rum, lemonade, and honey), and little glasses of beer.

As we dine at a palm-thatched restaurant, our waiter tells us about Santo Antao. It is the country's most beautiful island, he says, where fat mountains burst up from the center, cut by green valleys with sugar cane spilling out over the edges. The best part? Paradise is a mere one-hour ferry ride away.

We resolve to be at the dock at eight A.M., and continue shoveling in forkfuls of *cachupa*—the hearty corn-and-bean stew that everyone eats—though not everyone can digest.

But first we have to get aboard the Ribeira Ferry, an unexpectedly daunting task for those who aren't professional rugby players. We arrive at the dock just as the steward lifts the gangway rope to begin boarding. Immediately the two hundred-plus crowd morphs into a giant scrum, with everyone pushing, shoving, and elbowing their way to reach the entrance.

Why the rush? we wonder, as we watch grannies whack grown men with their canes and mothers with infants cat-fight for a place in line. The locals seemed so laid-back in the days prior, and now here we are, behind a woman who is siccing her chicken on people in a frantic bid to get to the front.

The answer becomes evident as the ferry chugs out of port, and our fellow passengers begin pulling yellow plastic bags out of their pockets, which they hold close to their mouths.

It turns out that where one sits on the Ribeira Ferry is of utmost importance. Sit on the lower deck, and there's a high risk of getting splatted on from the upper deck. Sit on the benches in the middle of the boat versus the benches on the perimeter, and there's less space and fresh air, which, were to become valued commodities in the minutes ahead.

We find ourselves on the top deck, middle bench.

Wish we could report it is the sea that's heaving during the short jaunt across the Atlantic, but it remains glassy. The Cape Verdeans, on the other hand, are heaving in alarming quantities.

The young boy across from us is the first to let loose. Alas, he has no plastic bag, and he urps at our feet. An elegant woman in a tan pantsuit beside him is next. She blows so gracefully into her bag that we aren't sure she's done so, until she raises her head and we see a chunk lodged at the corner of her mouth. A mother with her pre-school-age daughter curled in her lap sits to our right. The daughter is crying because she doesn't feel well, and the mother strokes her hair to sooth her. We expect big things from the little girl. However, it is the mom who hurls, craning her head away from the youngster and filling two bags.

And those are just the passengers in our immediate vicinity.

Cape Verdeans feed the fish from every corner of the boat. The air is punctured by sounds of *splat*, *burp*, and *gag* and by acidic smells. A quick glance at the floor leaves no doubt that *cachupa* really is the national dish.

We are at a loss to explain the cultural marvel that's been unleashed around us. Are locals born without inner ears? How can a culture that rides these boats on a regular basis— a culture of fishermen—be so seasick in calm waters? What will happen if there is a storm?

"Can it get worse?" I ask my partner.

"Depends on your outlook," he shouts above the din of our neighbors' unbridled belching. "Is your barf bag half full or half empty?"

We need to focus our thoughts elsewhere. Anything other than food and damp-browed Cape Verdeans will do. We settle on baseball batting averages as a safe subject for consideration, and by the time we've made it through the National League Central division, Santo Antao's port comes into view.

Then we feel it, like little drops of rain.

We aren't hit hard—that is the people on the lower deck—but our shoes and shorts are flecked. The teenage girl to our left, who has become greener and greener, can't hold it in any longer. She makes a dash for the railing and delivers a full-on lawn pizza, minus the lawn. The wind carries small pieces our way.

It is a relief to arrive on solid ground and shower. We

almost feel normal again, with good cheer restored after changing into clean clothes. Yes, we will have to get back on the Ribeira Ferry for the return trip. For now, though, we are safe on land, newly embarked in a minibus for the journey into Santo Antao's fabled mountains.

Until the man behind us pulls out a yellow plastic bag, and we realize our optimism is premature.

When she's not bouncing in bush taxis (Senegal), crashing in buses (Vietnam), extinguishing fiery cars (Latvia), and otherwise enjoying global transport, Karla Zimmerman sits at her desk in Chicago writing for Lonely Planet Publications, the Chicago Tribune, *in-flight magazines, and other publications.*

RIKKE JORGENSEN

* * *

The Adventures of Mega-Chicken

It's a showdown at the hoedown.

THREE HUGE FEATHERED CREATURES STARE ME DOWN, unafraid. Blue-black and barrel-shaped with incandescently red heads, they look me in the eye from ten feet ahead on the trail. I can only spot three, but I hear others fussing in the waist-high clutter of ferns beside me and see the under-growth shiver when they move.

"Beware," reads a sign on a tree trunk. "You are entering the breeding area of the Southern cassowary. This large, flightless bird defends itself aggressively by kicking with powerful legs, and can disembowel attackers with the dagger-like claws on its toes. The cassowary is an endangered species and must not be interfered with or harmed, under penalty of law."

Caught on the narrow trail, I am struck by the unfairness of it all. These birds might gut me like a freshly caught hal-ibut for coming too close, and what can I do? Take their picture. Even if I resolve to break the law in the name of self-defense, I can't very well fight my way through using my water bottle. I consider luring them off the trail with my lunch, then legging it, but reject that plan as hopelessly lame.

I have no idea what to do next. I've never before encountered life-threatening poultry.

In my native Denmark, the most dangerous animal you'd meet in the woods was a squirrel in a bad mood. But here in Australia, every creeper, swimmer, crawler, or slitherer is potentially lethal. Only weeks earlier, I had abandoned my safe and secure existence to travel to the Southern Hemisphere and be among wild things. I wanted to pit myself against Nature, to see if a different person would emerge: a stalwart alter ego that could never be born out of conference rooms and supermarkets and libraries.

I never expected to become someone terrified of super-sized chickens. But maybe I should have. Finding yourself in a strange, unknown world is

——) ——

My brain was telling me to run but I stood my ground. "For God's sake, it's just an eighteen-inch-high chicken," I told myself sternly.

It was my third day as a housekeeper-cum-handy-woman at Brindabella Station, a 300-acre cattle farm near Canberra. I hadn't realized I would live on the farm alone with just an arthritic dog, an adolescent cockatoo, and a killer cock-erel for company. Now I was face-to-face with that rooster and he was in a bad mood, having decided I was lusting after his chickens.

I eyed the cock warily and raised the large stick in my hand. "Don't make me use it," I warned, but it was too late, he charged.

◆

—Linda Christie,
"A Bird in the Hand…"

a potent trigger of fear and an easy way to lose all perspective—you're right back in your childhood room with the lights off, the monsters under the bed drooling for your blood. What's more, given enough time and leeway, fear will turn your brain to mush.

I knew I lacked Outback courage and I believed knowledge to be the next best defense, so before taking on miles of remote Australian rainforest trail with no ranger on hand to administer anti-venom, I made sure I was well informed. Clammy-handed, I had turned the pages of my wildlife guide to acquaint myself with red-bellied black snakes and brown tree snakes, the large, craggy wolf spiders, and the elegant golden orb-weavers. My body sticky with DEET, I hoped to repel not just insects, but venomous snakes and, if necessary, estuarine crocodiles.

Thus prepared, I reveled in the adventure as I set out alone to hike Daintree's tropical wilderness. I imagined that nobody had walked this route before me, at least not without machetes, not without an Aboriginal guide and a pack mule hauling fresh water. For the first mile or so, the hike merged seamlessly with my Discovery Channel dreams. The path zigzagged between giant, primeval trees with trunks like the legs of old elephants, deeply cracked and gray. Electric-green frogs sang from mossy rocks. Hand-sized yellow butterflies flitted drunkenly, inches from my face.

But as I labored deeper into the jungle, the set changed from charming and surreal to menacing. In a dim, silvery half-light I strained to check the ground in front of me for snakes. Emerald bromeliads became fewer and brushwood the blackish green color of old bruises dominated the view.

I thought about graves and maggots. With only a weak bit of sunlight penetrating the opaque canopy, the steamy heat was intense and claustrophobic. This was not a forest; this was the belly of a large beast. If I paused to listen, I could hear its wet, gargling breath.

My hands traveled around my body, brushing off real and imagined bugs. I walked into a spider's web. Feeling the invisible silky strands tickle my face and neck, I flew into a windmilling panic, hysterically swatting myself. After that, I held a defensive branch in front of me as I walked.

Every few minutes, a parrot's scream or the quick swish of a lizard scurrying across the path would make me jump. Even the flowers seemed alive with intelligent, carnivorous intent. Pink orchids the shape of rigid, fleshy lips shuddered as I went by. Clusters of flowers that hung from the canopy, tubular and openmouthed, drew me in with a sweet smell, then, when I leaned in close to sniff them, assaulted my nostrils with the stink of five-day-old meat. The path went from slender to anorexic and often I had to get on my back and squeeze under dense overhangs of wait-a-while vines, a climbing palm bristling with spines that will cut through leather.

Now, after five hours' struggle through this pungent sauna, three hungry-looking birds are eyeing me with apparent malicious purpose and I don't know what to do. But the decision makes itself when one bird struts forward with regal composure. After a deep breath and a quick brow swipe to get the drenched hair out of my eyes, both halves of the adrenal "fight or flight" reaction kicks in. I run and yell. Making noise, I hope, will both confuse the enemy and propel my escape velocity, so I howl like a dog with his tail caught in the door and gallop toward the birds. One quickly retreats into the brush, but two hold firm on the trail, seemingly taken aback by the development of events. Before they have a chance to kill me, I sprint between them. My arms brush against feathers and I catch a whiff of their sharp, foreign bird-smell, then I am gone, gasping toward safety.

I undertake the last mile in some triumph. I throw away the branch, daring spiders to attack at will. The thought of danger faced and dodged fills me with pride. I finish my water, certain that I will soon burst out of the eternal dusk into a world of brilliant sun and paved roads. Nature did its worst and I lived to tell the tale.

Much later, sipping peach iced tea in my hotel room in Port Douglas, I look up the cassowary in the wildlife guide. Apparently, this bird—a short-tempered cousin of the emu, capable of mauling grown men—stands six feet tall and has a bright blue head with a horny outgrowth. It is very rare indeed, and more to the point, looks nothing like the birds that accosted me back on the trail.

A few pages later, I come across a picture of my redheaded tormenters. The caption reads: "The common brush turkey is a friendly and curious bird that often approaches humans to beg for food. Please do not feed it."

Rikke Jorgensen is a Danish travel writer living in San Francisco whose work has appeared in a number of national newspapers. Rikke is addicted to dogs and well-worn jeans, she is a popcorn connoisseur, and she mispronounces a variety of English words.

ELIZABETH ASDORIAN

* * *

Midmorning Express

Who you gonna call?

AS SOPHIE AND I HUDDLED TOGETHER IN AN ISTANBUL apartment filled with freak-show rejects and pondered how we would fare in a Turkish prison (would the toilets be any better than the deep pits we had been hovering over for the past three weeks?), I kept replaying the words of a swarthy Mykonosian we met before we left Greece. "What the hell are you girls going to do in Turkey?"

Of course, "Fear for my life" wouldn't have been my first response. And as far as I know, the tourist pamphlets don't trumpet "hiding from drug-sniffing dogs." I longed to be innocently frolicking on the beach where Brooke Shields and that blond guy made out in *The Blue Lagoon*.

But somehow, we had met up with a Turkish Mafia don named Kaan. And now, we were just hoping to get out of the former Constantinople sometime sooner than thirty years-to-life.

It had started innocently enough. I had met Sophie, a giraffe of an Aussie, outgoing, fearless, and world-wise, in the

Cyclades. We had discovered our mutual love of booze, and after bucketloads of ouzo, she made a hard sell for the Aegean Coast in Southern Turkey.

"It'll be bonzer, darls!" she loudly announced, in that hopelessly confusing Australian way of shortening words and inventing others.

Now, I have never actually wanted to go to Turkey. On my list of "must-do" places, it ranks somewhere between rabbinical school and the Antarctic. My little old Armenian aunt, Auntie Rose, threatened to put a hex on me if I ever went near "those people." And I was none too excited about a Western woman's reputation in Turkish society (whores and witches, I think I heard).

"Bonzer?" It sounded vaguely ominous. "I don't want to be paranoid, but won't we be chased by angry mobs and stoned and called Western she-devils?"

"Come on now luv, don't throw a wobbly. We're not wussy Sheilas, are we?" Maybe Sophie wasn't, but I suspected it described me to a tee.

"Have you seen *Midnight Express*?" I asked her, wearily. "Besides, my *burka*'s at the cleaners."

"Oh, please," she sighed, "don't be such a whacker."

Whacker or not, I got on the damn boat to Turkey.

We made quite a pair as we trudged through the harrying Turkish custom's checkpoint in Kusadasi. There was giantess Sophie, flowing sunstreaked hair, golden skin, rich brown eyes, svelte and saucy—if she made Western men's knees weak, I was loath to imagine what she was doing to these ultra-repressed Eastern versions. Then there was me—a small, dull-haired human turtle with an enormous backpack humping my shoulders.

"You pay twenty dollars for visa. Kiss me, zero commission. No kiss, you pay extra," charmed the beady-eyed custom's guy. And he was the least misogynistic of the men we encountered.

I started tossing around wobblies like a double-jointed circus juggler.

"Sophie," I whined, "I already feel like a slab of chuck roast here."

Sophie, who, had she felt like meat, would have more likely been a nice chateaubriand, dragged on her cigarette and told me I was acting like a big girl's blouse.

"Just give it a burl," she commanded.

Oh, what was the use? I was thousands of miles from home, in a place where women had little more respect than a can of SpaghettiOs, stuck with an Amazon who not only attracted men like flypaper but could squash them just as easily. But I would give it a burl. I would give Turkey a friggin' burl.

So we traveled this place I was dead set on hating. But darn it, if it wasn't beautiful. There was lush green vegetation. Red craggy rocks. Disarmingly blue-green seas. Olive trees, all silvery and precise. We made our way through villages filled with centuries-old buildings, catching glimpses of children in dark-blue school uniforms and old men in woolen caps mindlessly fondling their worry beads or playing backgammon. Of course, the women were toiling in the fields with giant baskets on their heads, but it did have a certain charm, nonetheless.

And then, on the day before we were to head north to Istanbul, we met Kaan. Or Tom, as he liked to be called. We were in a crowded post office in Anatalya, staring blankly at the "great mystery phones," a group of mammoth orange monsters with no rhyme or reason to their usage.

Up walked Kaan, a stocky, melanic Turk, jovial and robust

and, by the enormous gold rings on his chunky hands, not lacking in the lira department. His decidedly Western attire certainly wouldn't have passed the mosque patrol—"Daytona Beach, Spring Break" screamed his faded beefy tee.

"You have the trouble making magic with phones?" he asked, rather sweetly. "I introduce you to the calling." And, in a gallant move we had not experienced in Turkey thus far, he tamed the evil orange monsters for us.

Our hero was immediately taken with Sophie. "Big girl, you are very tall and that is a thing that is nice. I give you food and drink from my pocket!" I hoped this meant he was buying.

After an amazing meal and gallons of *raki* (the Turkish equivalent of moonshine) paid for by our new best friend Kaan, he made another chivalrous move.

"Tomorrow, this Nuri ride to Istanbul the train of yours!" Kaan announced proudly. "You will be guest of the home of mine that lives there." Nuri, an angry, shifty-eyed teenager, grunted. I gathered he spoke no English; it was unclear if Nuri even had a tongue.

"That's aces, Tom," Sophie replied, happily.

But I had an uneasy feeling about the whole thing. "Sophie, it sounds kind of shonky to me," I said, hoping that speaking in Aussie vernacular would sound less wimpy than American girlish. "We don't know this guy. Don't you feel weird about staying in his house?"

"Oh, she'll be apples, darls."

But as I wandered off for the night, I passed Kaan talking to another traveler. It might have been all the *raki* I drank, but I could have sworn I heard Kaan say, "Bring the hash of mine to Cappadocia and you will eat your brains."

We arrived in Istanbul the next day; I was groggy and

disoriented and getting really peeved at my daisy-fresh, chipper sidekick. I was, however, secretly grateful for our mute tour guide Nuri; at least there wouldn't be the usual trauma of finding a place to stay.

Yet, as we followed him through the twisted streets and claustrophobic alleys of Sultanahmet, and the virtually unnavigatable Kumkapi district, the words "white slave trade" kept reverberating in my head. Was I going to be sold for a couple donkeys or a fertile camel? I wondered jealously how much more livestock Sophie would fetch.

We finally arrived at an apartment building, smelling a bit like livestock ourselves. Nuri led us to a modest flat and grunted. We followed him inside.

On the threadbare couch sat a small dark woman with a lazy eye. Both her wrists were heavily bandaged. Next to her were a young girl of about twenty and her boyfriend. The girl had no front teeth, and he seemed barely able to hold up his large head. The air was heavy with a nose-twitching smell; a giant hookah sat nearby.

"Tom said to be comforted here in this home that is his. Do you have an important meeting with water?" asked the toothless girl.

"Oh, you mean a shower?" I asked. A shower sounded heavenly. Stripping down with this odd harem nearby did not. "Actually, could we just take a nap?"

The toothless girl nodded and led us to a small room down the hallway. There were two beds, and best of all, a hearty lock on the door. I huffed as I sat on my bed.

"This place is weird." I thought I was stating the obvious.

"Oh, don't throw another wobbly," Sophie admonished. But I thought I heard a slight hesitation in her usually boundless bravado.

Against my better judgment, I fell into an unsettling sleep. When we woke, it was dark. And there was an exorbitant amount of hysterical yelling going on—more than I usually like in a strange house in a strange country.

The ruckus sent Sophie and me sprinting into the living room. There was Nuri, sweaty and out of breath with the other assorted oddballs barricading the door and darkening the windows. The old woman with the bandages was crumpled on the floor, praying to Mecca.

"What's going on?" I asked the girl with no teeth.

"Nuri was of the running," she muttered.

"What was Nuri running from?" Sophie queried in a frightened whisper.

"The men who are of the police had to the chasing Nuri."

I put my hands on my hips. "The police were chasing Nuri because…"

"Nuri buy the hashish," the girl said in a "well, duh" kind of way.

——— ☽ ———

Sartre once said that hell is other people. I would add to that, if other people are fat, sweating Germans with bad breath or deodorant-phobic Italians, and you're five-foot-two, claustrophobic, wearing a thirty-pound backpack, sweating like a pig yourself, haven't bathed in a while, and are jammed like a frigging sardine, standing up, on an overloaded bus in 85-degree heat on a torturously winding mountain road barely one-lane wide—and you pull your calf muscle trying to remain upright and not plunge through the doors to your death off a 1,000-foot sheer drop. Seriously. *That,* my friends, is hell.

◆

—Laurel Miller,
" A Whacking in Naples"

Gulp.

Sturdy Sophie burst into tears. Apparently, she had seen *Midnight Express* after all. And suddenly, I became the Amazon.

"Well, Sophie and I really have to run," I said, trying to seem nonchalant, as if I was always hiding from the Gestapo or the gendarme or the bobbies in foreign countries.

But the cult of Kaan firmly insisted we stay. Very firmly. Which left us two choices: remain here with the Turkish Munsters, or make a break for it into waiting hands of the police, who might gladly introduce us to the Turkish penal system.

I desperately tried to remember what Billy, the hash smuggler, did to free himself in the last minutes of that movie. Crap, why did I always fall asleep in the last minutes of movies?

So there we were.

Sophie had curled her lanky frame into the fetal position and was moaning quietly, "I'm such a dill."

I had to agree. But I'd be damned if I was going to be a dill, too. I'd been a passive patsy—a bloody ocker—my entire three weeks in Turkey. And despite my protests, I'd been lured to the lair of a drug overlord. I was mad as hell and I decided it was time to stop being a pushover and start being a badass.

So I plotted our midnight express (slang for escaping from prison, I recalled from the film). It was actually a midmorning express, but that's beside the point. I gave Sophie firm instructions; she nodded feebly. We were breaking out at daybreak and I was leading the charge.

Of course, it really wasn't as dangerous as it sounds—it seems that the flock of numbskulls in the other room had smoked all the hash they had procured and were passed out on the floor.

We stepped over Nuri and gingerly opened the door to freedom. Outside, there were no cops in sight. We breathed in the warm Istanbul morning air. The sunlight was dazzling.

Instantly, a kindly Turkish cab driver pulled up. He spoke perfect English.

"Where may I take you?" he asked politely.

"To the airport. Now. And I'll pay you exactly 110,000 lira." I liked how my voice sounded.

"Excellent, miss," he said.

And as we passed the gleaming Aya Sophia and the shimmering Golden Horn of the Bosphorus Strait, I felt empowered. Turkey wasn't a bad place; it just wasn't a place for me.

But I was leaving this country with a newfound appreciation of my inner super hero. I felt lucky to be leaving with such a profound discovery under my belt. Of course, later we would find out Kaan was indeed in the Turkish Mafia—he had tried to convince our friend Alex to smuggle counterfeit Byzantine statues to Italy—so I guess I was also lucky to be leaving with my life.

I turned to my friend, who seemed timid and delicate against the window of the Turkish cab.

"Hey Sophie," I asked. "Wasn't that bonzer?"

Elizabeth Asdorian is a freelance copywriter in San Francisco who peddles booze, computer chips, and tired technology magazines to consumers dazed by her sassy sales prose. Basing her literary fecundity on a complex formula of alcohol and calendar leap years, she has produced such unpublished classics as "The Blue Flu," "I Hate My Crazy Neighbor (No Sleep in the Dream House)," and numerous brilliantly executed angry letters to insurance companies. She also wrote a cartoon for the Daily Texan *with a really weird guy. Her dream is to write for a daytime soap opera, preferably* All My Children.

SUZANNE SCHLOSBERG

★ ★ ★

See How She Runs

It was a sprint to a Country Western beat.

IT WAS A COINCIDENCE PERHAPS UNPRECEDENTED FOR ANY
one family: On the very weekend that my cousin Mark participated in the Running of the Bulls in Pamplona, Spain, I
took part in the running of the tarps in Morristown, Ohio.

Less dangerous than the bull run but, I submit, no less
exhilarating, the tarp run is the stampede to claim prime territory for your lawn chairs at the Jamboree in the Hills, an
annual festival known as the Super Bowl of Country Music.

The Jamboree itself is a mesmerizing phenomenon: Every
July 100,000 country-music fans wearing cowboy hats and swim-
suits convene on an enormous grassy field, hauling custom-
made wagons loaded with coffin-sized beer coolers. I had
stumbled onto the event several years earlier while on a cross-
country bicycle tour and stayed for a couple hours, vowing to
one day return for the entire festival. This time I road-tripped to
Morristown with my Aunt Shari, the only member of my family back in Los Angeles who thought the Jamboree sounded like
fun rather than the worst vacation idea they had ever heard of.

I learned about the tarp run while standing in line at the porta-potties the afternoon before the show was to open and overheard two beefy men talking strategy.

"You gotta bunch up your tarp real tight to eliminate wind resistance," said the heftier of the two, sporting a Confederate-flag bandanna.

"Yeah, and you gotta focus really hard on the spot you want," offered the other guy, bursting out of a Harley Davidson t-shirt. "It's all about focus."

I asked what they were talking about and the confederate-flag guy, a veteran of nine Jamborees, gave me the lowdown. In short: each group designates a "runner," who wakes up before dawn to stand in line for several hours outside the concert venue. When the gates fling open, there's a mad rush toward the grassy field in front of the stage. Quickly unfurling your tarp, you stake your claim and wait for your backup team to arrive with the chairs, which you then plant securely on the tarp. The tag-team approach is essential because running with lawn chairs was outlawed a while back for safety reasons. "Some lady got whacked in the head," the flag guy explained.

With your territory secured, you stroll back to the campground, then return in the afternoon for the start of the show. You needn't worry about anyone messing with your tarp or your chairs, he assured me. "We all got respect for property rights."

Unlike the Pamplona bull run, the tarp run isn't something you do for kicks. It's a necessity. If you or your representatives don't participate, you can forget about getting a decent seat for the concert. Saunter over to the hillside when the stampede is over, one woman cautioned me, "and honey, you won't even find a place to put a Tic Tac on the ground."

I hadn't traveled so far just to find a seat in the next county. Besides, the whole concept got my competitive juices flowing and, as a bike racer, I appeared to be a bit more fit than the average Jamboree attendee. Aunt Shari was happy when I eagerly volunteered to be our runner.

I felt slightly less eager at four o'clock the next morning, when the alarm clock in our trailer buzzed. "Get us a good seat," Aunt Shari mumbled as she rolled over in her bed.

While I power-walked with my turquoise tarp in the darkness, my head pounding from four hours' sleep, I couldn't believe that I was waking up this early a) on vacation, b) for an event that wasn't going to start for ten hours, and, c) for a concert whose headliner's big hit was "She Thinks My Tractor's Sexy."

I zipped past a couple dozen people on my way to the nearest gate and upon arriving, around 4:30 A.M., was pleased with my position. There were only about fifty people lined up in front of me. Considering that at least two dozen of them were drinking beer, I figured my chances of success were good.

For the first two hours, the crowd was fairly low energy. Mostly we just lolled on the ground and slept. But as the sun began to crest over the hills, the crowd at my gate swelled to several hundred and I could feel the anticipation building.

Then suddenly it dawned on me: I had no idea which direction to run. As I eavesdropped on conversations, I realized people had very different ideas of a good seat. Some felt the closer to the stage the better, while others argued that sitting up front would make your eardrums explode. Some were touting a specific spot "about twenty-five feet behind the B section and thirty feet to the left of the C sign"—or something like that. I began to worry that experience counted more than fitness.

The task seemed even more daunting when I learned we would be running against a much larger stampede that would be released from the main gate at the top of a big hill. Having farther to run, the main-gate herd would be set free a few minutes before us and would be hurtling toward us at high speeds from a diagonal. "Watch out or you just might get broadsided," one woman warned me.

With fifteen minutes to go before the gates opened, a man in a pink shirt and a cow-patterned baseball cap appeared carrying a walkie-talkie. His name tag identified him as Denny Schwing, and he appeared to be in charge. At this point, the crowd had swelled to the thousands and was getting restless, chanting, "DEN-NY SCHWING, LET US IN! DEN-NY SCHWING, LET US IN!"

By the time Denny signaled his troops to open our gate, my brain was so crammed with advisories that I was hopelessly confused, not to mention a bit fearful. Instantly, thousands of bodies were hurtling across the field in every direction, as if someone had yelled "Fire!" only without all the screaming. Adrenaline pumping, I clenched my tarp in one hand and sprinted toward the front, center part of the grass, pumping my arms in a protective semicircle around me and exaggerating my knee lift so I wouldn't trip. I suspect I looked something like Richard Simmons doing high-impact aerobics.

Then suddenly, about thirty seconds into the run, I realized everyone around me was already whipping out their tarps. So I abruptly unfurled mine and pounced on it, without even assessing my position in relation to the stage. Breathless, I sat down to collect myself and was awestruck by the sea of tarps around me—and by my remarkable proximity to the stage. I appeared to be neither too close nor too far, though I wouldn't find out for sure until the concert started.

I promptly conked out and was awoken an hour later when Aunt Shari arrived with our lawn chairs. She was impressed with the parcel I'd secured, especially when the three women on the tarp next to ours said this was the same exact spot they'd gone after for eight consecutive years.

"Well, babe," Aunt Shari said, "looks like you're a natural."

That night, the crowd went nuts when Kenny Chesney sang about his sexy tractor. But personally, sitting on what had to be the best patch of grass in eastern Ohio, I felt like I was the star.

Until it dawned on me: If I wanted my seat back tomorrow, I was going to have to get up at four A.M. and do it all over again.

Suzanne Schlosberg is the author of Fitness for Travelers *and coauthor of* Fitness for Dummies. *Her latest book,* The Curse of the Singles Table: A True Story of 1001 Nights without Sex, *chronicles a celibacy streak that takes her to Iceland, China, Fiji, Alaska, and the Russian Far East.*

＊

Despite the fact that I'd just been camping with my family thirty one years ago, I joined four friends last month for a night at the West Point Inn, a ninety-six-year-old lodge on the upper south slope of Mt. Tamalpais. I packed only enough eyeliners to go with the four outfits I brought, and three changes of earrings. To my surprise, Mt. Tam requires no eye makeup, and I lived in the same outfit the entire time. In fact, it's still standing out there on my patio.

I had apprehensions about "roughing it," but as I sat in my friend's van on the way toward Stinson Beach next to lurching bottles of balsamic vinegar and olive oil, my fears of roasting hot dogs on sticks started to fade. In fact, it was more like *Bon Appetit* magazine, only with dirty socks. Maybe not everybody takes Kalamata olives on camping trips, but you need them for a Greek salad.

Apparently, you also need smoked trout, prawns with baby vegetables, and those cute little balls of chewy mozzarella.

For a non-camper, it was like heaven and hell rolled into one. The food and friends were great, the hikes invigorating, and the views stunning. But some aspects of the adventure were a bit off-putting. Like the mountain lion signs.

I've yet to run into a mountain lion while dropping the kids off at school, or at the underpants table at Victoria's Secret. The truth is, I like them best in dioramas. But they're out there, and they're not easily scared by jangling car keys.

And then there was the snake issue. I didn't know whether my cucumber-scented antibacterial hand gel would work as an anti-venin, and I was unsure about that business with the pocket knife and the blood-sucking. I didn't think I could cut that deep with an eyebrow tweezer anyway.

—Elaine Hamill, "I Came, I Saw, I Showered"

. ⋆ * ⋆

A Cowboy in Vienna

Choose your sidekicks carefully.

"Do I look like a Village Person?"

The Cowboy stood arms akimbo in front of Vienna's venerable Hotel Sacher just steps from the rococo entrance to Emperor Franz Joseph's State Opera House where the world's last great ball was about to begin. Actually, he looked more like Black Bart. He had agreed to rent a black tux and tails for the occasion, but insisted on wearing his hat and boots. Taking a cowboy to a ball was proving to be more of a gamble than I had imagined. My Inner Princess was about to pitch a royal fit.

All girls raised on Disney have an inner princess. And all inner princesses have an inner vision of going to the ball with Prince Charming. So when I received an invitation to Vienna's Opera Ball I said yes! yes! a thousand times YES! despite the fact that I hadn't met my truly regal husband yet and, at the time, there wasn't a prince...or even a good-looking pauper...in sight. Desperate, I settled for a friend-of-a-friend, a Montana cowboy who happened to have been born in Austria half a century earlier and swore he could still waltz and speak German.

"Voh est ein…ur..suitcasen?" The Cowboy asked the Swiss Air representative at the Vienna Airport.

"I assure you it will arrive on the next flight," she replied in the Queen's English, "and we'll deliver it to your hotel directly."

"I don't believe this!" The Cowboy hissed. "It was a non-stop flight. How could they lose my luggage?"

"They'll *find* it," I replied. "They're *Austrians*. I thought cowboys were supposed to be good in crises."

"I need a Schnapps," The Cowboy huffed, and stomped off to the airport bar while I went outside to hail a cab.

Apparently he was more genetically predisposed to his homeland's national drink than its language. This was unfortunate. Austrians offer Schnapps to all guests the moment they arrive anywhere, and all bars stock numerous versions of the strong Germanic *eau de vie*. By the time The Cowboy met me at the curb he was feeling no pain.

"If I was any happier I'd be twins!" he announced, then produced a burp so potent it made the taxi driver laugh.

"Schnapps?" he said, reaching for a bottle under his seat.

"Don' minden if ein do!" The Cowboy sang.

You can imagine my horror to learn that our hotel, the fabulous Palais Schwarzenberg, had mistakenly booked us in the same room.

"I'm so sorry," the desk clerk offered. "Naturally, we assumed…"

She could give me my own room the following night, but for now I was stuck with the schnappsified cowboy who immediately fell onto his side of the bed, pushed his hat down over his face and started making horse and donkey noises that outlasted the delivery of his lost luggage at five o'clock the following morning. By then the room smelled like a distillery and my inner princess was screaming "Off with his head!"

Exhausted, I dragged myself into the bathroom for a bubble bath. I had one foot in the tub when there was a knock at the bathroom door.

"Sorry, but you'd better make your sweet self scarce," said The Cowboy hoarsely, "Less'in ya'll wanna watch Wyatt Urp."

For years I have trained myself to look on the bright side of things. At least, I thought, I'm in Vienna. At

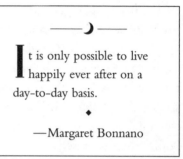

It is only possible to live happily ever after on a day-to-day basis.

♦

—Margaret Bonnano

least I'm staying in a genuine European palace. The Palais Schwarzenberg is a glorious 300-year-old remnant of Austrian aristocracy. Filled with museum-quality furniture and art, it still serves as the winter palace of the illustrious Schwarzenberg family. While The Cowboy slept off his hangover, I took myself to breakfast in the Palais's elegant dining room. My Inner Princess considered it a just reward when I was seated at the table next to Prince Schwarzenberg his Teutonic self. A dignified gentleman, the prince nodded in my general direction with the slightest suggestion of a smile as a young waiter served me tea in a silver teapot. There was a fire in the fireplace and a score of perfectly pruned rose bushes quaked delicately in the winter wind just beyond the window.

"Your toast," my waiter intoned as if it were a regal proclamation.

My Inner Princess purred.

"I reckoned I'd find you here! How'd ya'll sleep?"

The words burned into my perfect morning like brand-ing irons. Prince Schwarzenberg raised a royal eyebrow. The Cowboy was back.

"I. Thought. You. Weren't. Feeling. Well."

"Wasn't. Just needed to catch up on mah beauty sleep."

He licked a finger and pretended to slick down an eye-brow. Prince Schwarzenberg rose to leave.

"Oh, wait!" The Cowboy called after him. "*Ick lieben-zie das fruiten-zie und das brot, um, toastedzie mit*…oh, yeah!—but-ter!—same as English! *Und some kaffee*, too—black, I mean, *schvartz*…you know, ha! like this hotel!"

"I'll be sure to tell your server, sir," the prince replied coolly, then vanished.

"Austrians," The Cowboy scoffed. "They all got alps up their…well, would ya look at that!"

I followed his gaze to the glossy, wooden antique bar at the far side of the room, then to the shelves of elegant bottles above it.

"Now *that's* one serious schnapps selection!"

"It's eight in the morning!"

"When in Austria!" he sang and ordered a double.

Suffice to say our waltz lesson at the prestigious Elmayer Dance Academy that day was a sweat equity venture for the besotted Cowboy.

"No, no, sir," our instructor scolded. "Vee turn this way, not that."

"But that's plum backwards!" The Cowboy burbled.

"Yes, the Viennese valtz is danced counterclockwise, the opposite to your American version."

"Or more to the point, of our cowboy version," The Cowboy muttered.

"If you please, sir," said our instructor, and offered me his arm. Moments later we were gliding effortlessly around the room.

"You see," the instructor advised, "she is a lovely dancer. It is you who must learn to lead properly."

My Inner Princess curtsied. The Cowboy frowned.

"That ain't no waltz," he sneered. "That's a damn carnival ride. Any place a fella can get a drink around here?"

Despite my dubious date, getting dressed for the ball that evening was thrilling. First of all, I had the whole room to myself, The Cowboy having been moved down the hall despite his rally of protests. I also had a bone fide ball gown, rented at one of Vienna's finer dress shops. While the bath water ran, I laid my underwear and stockings carefully out on my bed then worked my hair into a French twist. Miraculously, it went up seamlessly on the first try. I spritzed it with a little bottle of Chanel #5 I'd bought at the Duty Free shop, a scent I'd always wanted to try that seemed just right for a ball. Once I was dressed, I sprayed some more on my décolletage.

"Perfect," I thought, then waited for The Cowboy to knock on my door as planned. He arrived half an hour late, reeking of schnapps and looking like a riverboat gambler. My Inner Princess hollered "Off with his hat!" When I ducked into the bathroom to refresh my lipstick I saw them. Spread across my chest like an angry army. Welts. Blistering red welts. I was allergic to Chanel #5, or, perhaps, cowboys.

At the Opera House, we were greeted by the European paparazzi, and the 150,000 Italian roses that decorated the foyer. Stanzas of Viennese waltzes rushed in from the orchestra anytime anyone opened a door to the main ball room, while scores of gloriously dressed couples floated up and down the Opera House's *Gone With the Wind* Grand Staircase, aromatic comets of Guerlain and Jean Patou pirouetting in the air around them. One woman really did look like a princess in a dress of white silk satin dotted with hand-made pastel silk rosebuds, her soft blond curls bobbing as she moved. Closer inspection revealed a classically beautiful face held together by the handiwork of an excellent surgeon…but who cared!

The Cowboy and I charged up the Grand Staircase, a broad marble miracle lit up by chandeliers that was one of the few parts of the Opera House to survive a direct bomb hit in 1945. Many stairways later, we reached the upper balcony where we had been told we'd find our seats. "No, no," said the usher. "Zeez are special tickets, on zee dance floor stage downstairs."

Back down we ran. And ran and ran, showing our special tickets to anyone with a flashlight and a badge. "No, no—zat

---

—) —

On a recent trip through Arizona, I stopped at a rest stop to use the ladies' room. Imagine my shock when, exiting the stall, I was face to face with a rather tall man. I don't know which one of us was more surprised.

"Looks like you're in the wrong one," he said, trying to make the situation a little less uncomfortable.

"No, you are," I told him after checking the outside of the door to be sure it said LADIES.

He looked embarrassed, but at the same time tried not to smile as he said, "Well, if I am, then so is my wife."

♦

—Mauverneen Blevins,
"Gender Jumble"

way," the official would say, and off we'd go. For the next hour we ran, literally, through the Opera House's astounding catacomb of side chambers and hallways, and missed completely the breathless entrance of the ball's 140 debutantes in white gowns and tiaras clinging to their nervous young gentlemen. We missed their traditional polonaise (a triple-meter promenade of Polish origin), their opening ballet, and their First Dance, after which the rest of the attendees are invited to join the First Waltz. Thousands of gleeful Viennese flooded the dance floor sweeping us along with them. I was sweaty, my hair was hanging in my face, my chest looked like the Creature from the Histamine Lagoon, and my feet were killing me...but my Inner Princess was in heaven. This was Vienna! And despite my decidedly unprincely escort, this was an honest-to-God European ball. At that moment, much to the amusement of our fellow dancers, The Cowboy swung me into a nauseating Western waltz, his ridiculous boots clicking madly on the old wooden dance floor. The women giggled at his hat and the men clapped him on the back, then a television commentator turned her camera on us and pointedly asked the Cowboy:

"Und how did you find zee ball?"

He stopped, grinned, tipped his hat and said: "I just followed the herd, m'am. I just followed the herd."

Jessica Maxwell wanted to be a serious environmental reporter until her first assignment, on the Los Angeles sewer system, went south when she learned that the treatment plant's supervisor was named Arthur F. Suher. She is the author of books on golf, fly fishing, and international travel, and continues to write for magazines specializing in what she calls the "literary culinary conservation sporting travel narrative." She lives with her trial attorney husband and part-bobcat kitty in Eugene, Oregon.

JENNIFER L. LEO

* * *

Squeaky Clean, and Then Some

*Grimy single women in their thirties smelling
like trains can't be choosers.*

SURROUNDED BY PILLOWS, HOOKAHS, AND THE SMELL OF burning candles, I barely noticed that the man serving me tea and butter cookies was only wearing enough fabric to cover his manhood. He looked like he had just walked off the movie set of *Troy*—but my eyes were peeled for a big burly babushka wearing a frown of hygienic seriousness.

I had the built-up grime of three weeks of European train travel, and was in dire need of a good scrubbing. I understood from the many stories I'd read that nothing would get me cleaner than a traditional Turkish bath or *hamam*. So what if I was in Munich and not Istanbul? A *hamam* is a *hamam* is a *hamam*—right?

I wolfed down my cookies, knocked back the tea, and thumbed through the stack of signed guestbooks piled in front of me. I couldn't read the German, but one English inscription said, "Hassan was wonderful!" The big bubbly handwriting reminded me of girlish crush notes passed in high school history class.

Just then, Johnny Square Jaw returned and led me down-stairs into a steamy warren of cavernous rooms. He gave me a locker and handed me a miniskirt the size of his own before disappearing. I undressed, wrapped the fabric around my butt, and gave my naked boobs a celebratory jiggle. The cost of my *hamam* experience was ten times what one would pay in Turkey, but I expected that from traveling in pricey euro-land.

I walked down the hall eager to discover what was next and was taken aback when my bare-chested stud introduced himself as Hassan. O.K. then, this should get interesting.

Hassan left me in the shower room. I hung up my wrap and reached for the bath gel. Why was *I* showering? Wasn't I paying *him* to get me clean? Before I could figure it out, he was standing before me expressionless—seemingly unaffected by my complete wet nudity. Without expla-nation he took my hang-ing loincloth and reached around my waist to wrap it around me. His arm brushed against my hip, and I knew this would be unlike any spa treatment I'd had at Bellagio in Las

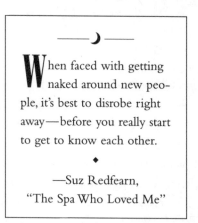

When faced with getting naked around new peo-ple, it's best to disrobe right away—before you really start to get to know each other.

♦

—Suz Redfearn,
"The Spa Who Loved Me"

Vegas. I started to walk that fine line between feeling vulner-able because he just saw *everything*, and having the strongest urge to immediately call all the girls back home!

We settled into a large tiled room with steamy corners and a dark starlit ceiling. It was clean and had the calming ambi-ence of other upscale spas I'd indulged in, with one excep-tion: handsome Hassan.

He poured bowls of warm water over me, brushed it off my eyes with a lover's touch, and led me to the warm stone table. I lay face up and relaxed while Hassan started with a scalp and shoulder massage. Then he pressed his palm up the center of my chest between my breasts. I had to wonder what technique he was using. Was this Turkish, German, or perhaps the international style of any man within inches of a nearly naked woman? Hassan's bowling straight up the middle was something else. Maybe he was straightening my chi. The only men who had previously touched me like this had their own parking space in my heart and smelled more like sporty deodorant than Dead Sea salts. I was curious to see if his hands would throw a gutter ball, so I kept still and waited.

When I opened my eyes, Hassan was staring wistfully back at me.

"Good?" he asked.

"Yes, *very* good," I replied, giving him the thumbs up. But I was really thinking, *freak!* Yes, the massage felt nice, but what was with the mooning looks? Or maybe I needed a black light to read the writing on the wall. Hassan *would* make an excellent babe slave. So good that I got a little concerned. What exactly had I just paid for?

More importantly, what exactly *could* I pay for? My needs went way beyond a German bratwurst. How about a one-way ticket home to be my beck-and-call boy? All he needed was some clothes. No more wasting time in long lines at the coffee shop. I could dig right into checking my e-mail while Hassan fetched the lattes. Working late? No worries, Hassan is home whipping up a seafood risotto. Like to roll the bones? Hassan is a gambler, too! Did I mention he plays guitar? Oh yes, just add water and Hassan magically transforms into Eager to Please Man. Accessory tool belt sold separately.

I had just found the mecca for lonely single women everywhere. Speed dating—what a laugh. Table for Six? Not anymore. Just get yourself over to Munich for a massage and see what happens next.

It was now time in the treatment package for the Soap Massage. Hassan lathered and kneaded my legs while I closed my eyes and let my mind travel out of Germany. His hands on my back were even more relaxing than the front. I could have enjoyed just this for the remaining hour if it weren't for the warm air beating on my face. What could that be? I opened my eyes and found Hassan's smiling face an inch and a half from mine. What was he doing? Was he waiting for me to kiss him? Freak Eyes had returned.

I took my friend Katy to a burlesque show in San Francisco, and all I have to say is that if I'm paying $25 for a ticket, I expect a little more T&A.

◆

—Jennifer Colvin, "Saturday Night in the City"

I hadn't ordered any extras. I felt like laughing, but didn't want to offend him. What did other women do? Could you get an upgrade just by leaning in a little? He was still there. Still smiling. If he stayed that close I could whisper my fantasies of sending him to Kinko's. I was in the hands of a German-Turkish multi-tasker. If Hassan had the ability to massage my soapy back, and keep his face within inches of mine, surely he could balance making color copies and filling out a Fed Ex form. Now that's the kind of service that makes me hot.

Hassan motioned me to flip sides again. I thought we'd already covered that territory, but apparently there were even more suds to spread. A thick lather billowed on my chest. Lefty and Righty stood at attention. They did that all on their own. Geez, did he notice? Of course not, I was in *his* office. If he saw 4 naked women in a day, that's 80 in a month, 960 in a year after vacation and sick leave. Nearly 2,000 naked boobs of varying shapes and sizes.

It was time, I had thought about it before, but now I had the guts. Boner check. I looked over the edge of the table at his multi-colored wrap. No protrusion. Damn skirts, it'd be so much more obvious if he were in sweats. I made sure he wasn't playing loverboy staring contest again, and went in for another inspection. Still nothing. Was he gay? Or was I just another door panel on the 2005 Ford Focus? Oh great, "Schlameal Schlamazel Hazzen Pfeffer Incorporated." There was

I'm tired of all this nonsense about beauty being only skin-deep. That's deep enough. What do you want, an adorable pancreas?

◆

—Jean Kerr

no way I would get the theme song to *Laverne and Shirley* out of my head now.

Hassan held my hand and there were only bubbles between us. His hands flowed as one up and down my back while he held me in his arms. Again we were face to face. He looked deep into my eyes, the edges of his mouth starting to curl upwards. All I could muster was, "This is the cleanest I've ever been!"

He looked puzzled. Did he understand my English? I said it again.

I really didn't know what I was supposed to do. I wasn't

interested in sex. I wanted a man who knew how to carve a turkey. Wait, no, that's jumping ahead to a different desire altogether. I was here to get a traditional Turkish scrub.

Hassan backed up and took me to the other side of the bench. It was time to wash my hair. Just when I thought things couldn't get any weirder, he walked to my front and began tickling my ears. Soapy towel in each auditory orifice.

Then he pointed to the garden hose hung on the wall.

"You want?" he said.

Excuse me? Did he think I was a car? I laughed and shook my head. I was done.

Now it was my turn to sign the guestbook. I flipped through the previous entries and found more girlish bubbly writing: "Magic Hands!" "Pleasure Palace!"

"Highly recommended," I scrawled in the book. And then I thought—for drawing a bath, taking out the dry cleaning, getting the mail, beer runs, dumping the trash, changing nasty diapers, and making your friends drool at cocktail parties.

Jennifer L. Leo won an underwear contest her freshman year at USC during a traditional drumline hazing ritual in the Trojan Marching Band. She spends her time traveling, writing, editing, and is the author of a popular online blog for travel writers called writtenroad.com. She is the editor of this book as well as the award-winning Sand in My Bra and Other Misadventures.

*

My sister showed up the other day with a new set of breasts. Bouncy breasts. Rounded breasts. Breasts that aim dead ahead with the resolve of a heat-seeking missile.

And I don't get it.

This is a woman so pathologically modest that she'd sooner be shot than be seen in her flannel, lumberjack-plaid lingerie, much less (no way!) stark naked. And yet here she is: lifting her top so all assembled—her husband, children, sisters, brothers, parents, in-laws, and dog—can witness the implant surgeon's handiwork. Braless, her breasts are mottled black and blue and brazenly shout hurt and pain. My sister beams.

"I don't mind showing everyone," she says, "because they aren't me."

Her husband Michael, feeling accused by the silence in the room, puffs for confrontation. "Trust me," he says, "I had nothing to do with it."

Dressed as usual in baggy blouses and camouflage sweaters and men's shirts that swing unisex, Camille's new breasts are utterly uninterested in flaunting their fresh and oh-so-fetching femininity. Apparently, their power is more subtle; their wiles less expected. In fact, my sister's fuller, firmer new friends are about to change her life. They will take her places she hasn't been in years, introduce her to adventures she never dared try. Once the incisions heal, the tenderness lessens, and they feel more at home on her chest, Camille's new breasts will turn her into the kind of traveler I barely dare to dream of being. A woman freer. Emboldened. Gutsier, if bustier.

For instance, my sister's magical new mammaries will inspire her to climb Alaska's Mt. McKinley, at 20,320 feet. And then complete the Ironman Triathlon in Hawaii. They will see her fly to the Bahamas for a romantic eleventh anniversary, plan a summer sojourn to Sweden, save for an African photo safari. Here a trip, there a trek, everywhere an airport security check...why, my sister's intrepid breasts will see to it she henceforth renounces routine and makes her life fun.

—Colette O'Connor, "Make Mine Me"

KALPANA MOHAN

* * *

Flora and Fauna
in Madrid

Everyone got more than they bargained for.

WE COULD HAVE SQUEEZED HER INTO THE BACK OF OUR four-person Peugeot hatchback. But our seven-year-old might have whined about sharing his seatbelt with a topless thing clad in just a red fig leaf.

The long-legged young woman twenty yards ahead of us certainly broke the green monotony of Madrid's famous park.

She protracted her ivory-colored back toward us, her pencil-thin legs making an almost obtuse angle with the asphalt. Perhaps Pythagoras would have salivated at the degree of the thigh-angle?

She stood there waiting for her prey, her right arm outstretched. Her thumb was turned up towards the peeking sky.

From where I sat in the passenger seat, I figured that if all she wanted was a ride in our economy rental car, she needed a wee bit more than skin-colored wires holding up the equivalent of an eye-patch where Eve normally wore her leaf.

At such a critical point on the road screeched a question that parents of young kids dread.

"Mom, why isn't that lady wearing a real *jetti*?"

Our seven-year-old had asked a simple enough question. *Jetti* is a Tamil word meaning panties. His voice rose higher as he repeated his question to seemingly deaf parents.

It certainly was higher than it was the week before when he sat and sunned by a million topless women on the sands of Cannes.

It had an I-know-this-woman-isn't-just-tanning ring to it.

Before we could address his question, a pack of women in colorful stages of undress popped up on a grassy knoll on our right.

My husband chose the right time to pick up one thing. An argument.

"Great, we've landed in the thick of a pick-up joint. Why on earth can't you learn to read a map?"

My tongue was about to hiss back when he yelled, flummoxed by another vision reeling in toward us on our left.

"Duck, kids!" he screamed, expecting his two children to obey. I tried holding their heads down. But given where I was sitting, it was like forcing two zero-spring, iron jacks back inside a jack-in-the-box.

The army of girls by the huge boulders in the clearing had patches of black on key body parts. Some were perched on the rocks. Some were standing by them, trying to wave us down, their sloppy grins promising kinky times. As our car neared them, a handful spun around, making eye-popping gestures about things that you'd never imagine possible unless you hung out for an after-dinner latte at Bangkok's Patpong.

"Dad, what's a pick-up joint?" Our eleven-year-old daughter chimed in between our outbursts, trying hard to keep her brother's head down while she took in the view.

Our son, who'd claimed he was tired of looking at yet

another architectural marvel in Madrid, kept coming up for air on this ride. Now he told his sister where to look.

"Look, *Akka*, that one way on the right's wearing a black top but it isn't covering her you-know-whats."

My son was right. The creature in the black halter had swung around. Her leather halter bolstered her enormous bosom but the cover was missing. And then she began juggling them, as if to say, "One...Two...What shall I do? Three...Four...Oh what a bore." Another one in a black belt and a strategic V shook her behind so hard I was afraid she'd shake the cones out of the conifer tree shading the rocks.

We dodged this rowdy bunch and reached a fork on the road. A group of women swooped down from behind a clump of trees to the car at our left. Stop signs. How I hated stop signs that afternoon. The three boys in the ambushed car argued loudly, flashing notes to the bees that swarmed around the windows. At that moment, we were ready to pay a king's ransom to release us from nature's harem.

"So what do these women do, Dad?"

Our daughter earned As at school for persistence.

"You don't need to know. And I thought I told you *both* to have your heads *down*?"

Dad's tone was getting crabbier. The way it got when he was lost *and* perilously low on gas. Madrid's map was splayed wide open before me, but it wouldn't help us find the *salida* from this maze of sin.

We had come upon it while looking for the Jardines del Campo del Moro, the gardens by the Royal Palace of Madrid. At some point we'd found ourselves forced into a neverending tunnel. Then there was light. Like most clueless passengers who grab on to any straws to help a direction-challenged driver, I'd found my sign by the light at the end of the tunnel.

"Ah, there, the coming exit says Casa de Campo. So there, take this exit."

I'd folded the city map with short, snappy strokes, to show my husband how I'd saved us—once again. I'd sat back regally in a tight, unforgiving huff so he could see what a big deal he had made about getting lost.

We'd then sped through an unpretentious driveway into the royal grounds, relieved that we were going to be a whole family once again. On the right, we'd spotted happy families running around what seemed like a lake. Farther down, a man in a t-shirt and shorts was washing his car with a hose, hardly the sort of thing you'd expect to see inside royal grounds. But it didn't matter, around us the trees met the sky and it was going to be a beautiful day, after all.

Until we'd stumbled upon the thing in a thong.

Fifteen minutes into

—— ☽ ——

My two daughters—our first trip to Europe to-gether. Romantic visions of an era when every young woman's education included the grand European tour, swirled in my mind's eye like scenes from *A Room with a View*. Yet, as a diligent customs official pulled my eldest daughter aside to inspect her bag, the zipper sprang undone, releasing clothes that moved like a live animal. A long feather boa, two hardcover coffee table books, and a jumbo box of condoms rendered us speechless. "She is twenty-three years old. You should be proud that she is so responsible," said my youngest. Travels with family—is it always an adventure?

◆

—Michele Peterson,
"Travels with Mom"

hooker skirting, our daughter still wouldn't quit. Now she nudged me for explanations.

"So, Mom, Dad said a word. 'Pick up' or something. What's that?"

"These women are trying to attract men."

"How weird. In such clothes?" She rolled her eyes and sat back.

I sighed. I'd finally detected a full stop to her questions. But our son piped up.

"Why, why are they trying to attract them?"

"For money. Just some bad girls who do favors for men."

Now we were at another intersection in the road. My husband decided to make a left. I prayed momentarily—for deliverance from sin and for a gas station.

The signs for Madrid came up. But one question remained to be answered even as we entered the highway into the city and spotted the signs for the nearest gas station.

"Mom, what kind of favors?"

Kalpana Mohan has one bit of advice to offer travelers in Europe: Take the train. A train knows where it's going, keeps family members at a civil distance, abhors red light districts, and never rattles into a minuscule parking garage where the entryway is also an exit. Kalpana's work—on topics ranging from technology to parenting and ethnic issues—has appeared on NPR, Business Week Online, *in the* San Jose Mercury News *and* Bay Area Parent, *among others.*

LYNN SANTA LUCIA

* ✳ *

Miami Spice

Ditching the boss as Olympic sport.

IT'S MIDSUMMER IN MIAMI. BOLD COLORS, BLINDING WHITE, and blazing sun stop me in my path. Heady fragrances— hibiscus, coconut oil, an unidentifiable briny-sweet something born of ocean and lush landscape that if bottled would be named *El Calor de Amor* or *Pasión Tropical*—confound my senses. The oppressive heat weighs like a damp, steaming bathrobe around my shoulders, practically forcing me to my knees.

At five in the afternoon, clusters of beach-goers rise up ever so slowly from rumpled towels and make their way across the sandy stretch from shoreline to ocean boardwalk like sluggish sea turtles in search of shade and liquid refreshment. I should be joining my boss (Manhattan's Ogre Editor Extraordinaire, who makes Sigourney Weaver in *Working Girl* look like a pussycat) and my co-worker (a twenty-year-old gay Adonis). But they think I'm nursing a crippling headache in my hotel room. "Lack of sleep." "The early morning flight." "Nerves," are the excuses I provide, referring to the trip in from New York and a deal-making meeting with one of the major cruise lines that lasted half the day. But, really, I need a break from these two. "I'll see you at breakfast," I tell them, forcing a smile. The boss looks let down. Adonis is not to be fazed.

And so, I'm on the beach, at Tenth Street, making a languid weave around stacks of plastic beach chairs and discarded bottles of Evian water, when I notice the cocky pitch of his head. One hundred yards in front of me, a sable mop of thick, shiny hair tapering to a serpentine finish at his nape seems to say, "Try me if you can handle the sting."

His back is bare, glistening with sweat and suntan oil, the color of a copper penny. His buttocks—high and round like a pair of perfect mangoes under knee-length shorts—appear ready for picking. And then, without warning, there's a shout. His arms jolt up in the air. He spins around and starts jogging toward me in pursuit of a wayward soccer ball. He runs with his head down, letting his loose hair flop across his face, and only when he notices a set of painted toes curling in the sand beside the immobile ball does he lift his gaze and look straight into my eyes. In an instant, my pulse is charging like cavalry. His cobra eyes—flashing like obsidian in the sun—stretch across his face and follow the pattern of his plump lips curled into a roguish grin. Words desert me. I see in the way he scrunches his forehead that he reads my silence as a challenge. So, I take advantage of the misinterpretation when he makes a move to retrieve the ball.

"That'll cost you," I say.

He stops mid-way, straightens up and gives me a deliberate look.

"Is that right?" he says.

I blink once, at half speed. "That's right."

We are like two stage actors, reading our parts for the first

time, not sure where the dialogue is headed and more interested in experiencing the flow. Time slows. He hooks a
thumb on his elastic waistband and slides it lazily from belly-
button to hipbone and back again. I secure a loose curl
behind my ear. From down the beach, a fellow teammate
calls out: "*Vamos!* Let's go!" He stretches his chin over his
shoulder like a cat that can't be bothered, and when he turns
back something clicks between us. We enter into a conspir-
acy of attraction.

"Where are you staying?" he asks.

I cock my head in the direction of Ocean Drive's string of
Popsicle-colored hotels appearing soft and vaporous in the
muggy air. He lands his eyes on a six-story structure with
portholes for windows and reads the rounded characters aloud:
"Tides," he says. Bull's eye. But I remember my co-workers.

"No. That's not it," I lie. I hesitate. The rolodex of South
Beach hotels in my head fast forwards. Then I tell him, "The
Delano, over on Collins."

Now his teammates are losing patience. A unified cry
explodes: "Come on, man!"

He scoops up the ball and stares into my eyes as if filling
them up with molten lava. "I'll meet you there at seven,"
he says.

The sun rests low in the sky and casts soft shadows around
the Delano's fantastic lobby with its built-in touches of madness: a vodka bar made to resemble an airy country kitchen;
conversation nooks bedecked with gilt candelabra. Past sky-
high white curtains that billow in the winds off the Atlantic,
I've found a cool spot up at the bar, seated beneath a circling
ceiling fan slicing air so thick it's drinkable.

The bartender approaches and serves me—his only customer—a Cosmopolitan the color of my flushed cheeks. I know I'm looking decidedly urbane sipping Miami's drink-of-the-moment in a strapless mini dress and oversized tinted sunglasses indoors. But, the calm, cool exterior is no cover for my smoldering core. The young bartender knows somthing's cooking. As he busies himself with a collection of vodka and rum bottles, he keeps his heavy-lidded eyes locked on me and cranes his neck each time I uncross and re-cross my bare legs. I turn my back on him to avoid any dialogue, but it's of no use.

"Where you from?" he asks.

I'm not sure what to answer. It's only been a few months since I moved from Miami to New York and, though I'm not originally from here, it's hard to grasp my new role of out-of-town visitor.

"Kansas," I finally say, feeling in the make-believe world of South Beach a bit like Dorothy in Oz, anyway.

The bartender raises an eyebrow questionably, his expression adding a decade to his twenty-odd years.

The clock on the wall reads a quarter past seven. My stomach does a back flip. I wonder where my beach beau could be. But, here, the world is on Latin time, so I remind myself that I can expect him to be at least twenty minutes late.

"How about some music, some Latin jazz…Manny," I say, reading the bartender's name off the tag pinned to his yellow *guayabera*, his Cuban-style shirt that's all pockets and plunging neckline.

"Oh," he says, "I got something you'll love."

I wonder if he's cooing about a compact disc from the assortment that's strewn behind the bar or about the something else that's unmistakable under his tight pants. It's a habit—this packaging of statements in sexual cellophane—to which I've become accustomed around the ravishing young singles who've helped establish this city's sizzle. He moves like honey over to the sound system.

"Turn it up," I say, as his arms with basketballs for biceps reach for the controls of the CD player. He looks my way, winks. And then, into the heavy air spills a sound that brings to mind hundreds of bare thighs swishing and crossing each other in Dionysiac splendor. When I ask Manny what it is, he describes what he calls *chequerés*, hardened gourds covered with hundreds of tiny shells and seeds embroidered in a net. He says they are the feminine equivalent of drums and I believe it, as the evocative whish and rustle of what now sounds like water, jungle, and sex start me swiveling on my barstool. It's at that moment I spot my boss being escorted through the lobby to an available table in the dining area just behind me. I crumple over my martini glass.

> ──── ☽ ────
>
> I've tried several varieties of sex. The conventional position makes me claustrophobic and the others give me a stiff neck or lockjaw.
>
> ◆
>
> —Tallulah Bankhead

"Is everything all right?" Manny asks.

"What do I owe you?" I say, fumbling in my purse, peeking up between the curls I've let fall across my face.

"You can't go now. Listen," he says.

A pulsing, unrestrained rhythm—a stimulating and haunting fusion of *chequeres*, timbales, congas, and flute—erupts from the stereo speakers, sending the bartender's hungry hips around the bar and traveling to the edge of my stool. He takes my hands and slides me onto my feet.

"Wait. Really. I can't," I say, my hands still locked in his. In an effort to keep my head lowered, my face out of my boss's sight, my cheek lands on Manny's chest. He moves my hands to his shoulders, cups his hands around my hips, and eases me away from the bar. I'm stunned into silence. It doesn't matter that we say nothing, because an animated dialogue has broken out between riotous timbales, congas, bongos, and bass, and he gets me moving in time to the frenetic rhythm, stepping and spinning around his toes and in and out of his arms. I give in to the music. The bongo-conga chatter continues. Then, a bleating trumpet and wailing sax break in, culminating in a full-blown rumba with all the trimmings and no holds barred. We step and spin and rattle our hips and when the last bata drum beats and the horns trip into silence I throw my head back and let my hair spill out behind me and shriek with laughter and total abandon. And then I take off for the ladies' room.

In the restroom, I catch my breath and count to sixty, expecting my boss to come in at any second. When the door finally opens, a full five minutes later, in walk two waif-like models, vying for space before the mirror. I still haven't figured out what to do next, but I know I can't stay in there, with the waifs in stilettos sizing me up between swipes of mascara.

I push open the door and let it swing shut behind me. I straighten my dress and take a deep breath. I peek around the corner of the alcove, trying to gauge how best to navigate my way back to the bar, to Manny, in order to leave him a note for my beach beau, without my boss seeing me. But before I can pull a pen from my purse, the door to the men's room flies open and out steps…guess who?

"Hello," we say over the still riotous jazz, locking eyes and not moving.

I have a sudden urge to fling the contents of the glass he's holding over our heads to experience a pink splash of relief in this shower of burning musical notes, but I bring the drink to my lips and take one long sip instead. He leans into me. *"Tu huele de coco,"* he says in my ear. My hip, slightly higher than his, curves neatly into his waist. His lips brush up against my neck. Again, he tells me, softly and in Spanish, that I smell like coconut.

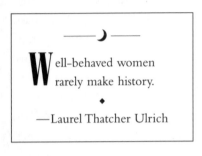

Well-behaved women rarely make history.

◆

—Laurel Thatcher Ulrich

I raise my arm at the elbow and crook my finger to indicate that he should follow as I make my way toward the back of the dining area. My boss is nowhere to be seen, but her table has not been cleared. Down the terrazzo-tiled steps of the terrace we go, where, out back, prized two-story bungalows surround a palm-lined infinity pool. At a poolside palm tree rising twenty feet from the concrete ground as if that were the natural thing to do, I stop and turn and lean my back against its trunk to steady myself for what I sense is to come. Sure enough, the sight of him alone, his tawny loveliness, turns me into jelly. His skin glows that post-sun, after-shower glow and his hair is slicked back in wetness. He wears black—a snug t-shirt, loose linen pants, stylish leather sandals—like eternal night. I feel his eyes piercing through me and I'm forced to leave it all up to him. But I can't. Because, right then, my boss steps out onto the terrace with a drink in her hand. Thankfully, she's gazing over the hotel property, to the beachfront beyond.

I grab my beach beau by the collar and swing him around a man-size chess piece and behind an enormous mirror punctuating this Wonderland-esque garden/pool area. I'm giddy, trembling, suddenly too shy to catch his eyes, and hurrying to recompose myself, because I'm sure this stranger whose name is still a mystery by now must think I'm a psychopath. Thankfully, he wraps his arm around my waist, imagining this is all in good fun. I crane my neck around the mirror. My boss just will not leave.

When the boss finally takes a seat at one of the terrace tables, exposing mostly her back to us, I make my move. Next door resides the Raleigh, another art deco hotel-for-hipsters, where Desi Arnaz once played the drums and Esther Williams swam in the pool. I take my mystery man by the hand and say, "Come with me," maneuvering him along the furthest edges of the Delano's property until we slip through an opening and find ourselves on the grounds of the Raleigh and in front of the most enticing swimming pool on the planet. He turns my body into his and we bask in the violet dusk, with the swimming pool a silver mirror framed by Rococo curlicues and flourishes beside us. We are very much alone. I catch a sudden whiff of his cologne. Intoxicated by his smell, I kiss him full on the mouth, taking his face in my hands and pressing his cheeks so that his lips become full and round between mine. *"Que maravilla,"* he moans.

We still can hear the music from the Delano. It is now sweet and promising, with flute, piano, and violins revealing their best, and I remember a Cuban phrase that defines the essence of the *danzón*: *"Que el relajo sea con orden"*: Let's have an orderly disorder. My hands move across his chest. One arm steals around my ribs, when a set of voices comes tumbling across the pool and stuns me out of my reverie.

"Miami is the kind of place," I overhear, "that makes people more than they really are."

We are quivering, breathless, suspended on an endless edge.

"It really is possible, here," says another, "to fall apart and be rendered completely unfit for normal urban life ever again."

Oh, the naked promise in his look. He lifts me up and sits me on top of an ardent impressionist dream of tangled vines and pink hibiscus spilling over a low white wall. We slip over the wall and on to the beach, expecting to put orderly disorder to the test.

Lynn Santa Lucia is a fervent traveler and storyteller. She believes that the best travel experiences happen in pursuit of a passion. Her writing—on everything from mangoes and motorscooters, luxury train travel and spiritual retreats—has appeared in Travel Holiday, Destinations, *and* Departures. *She recently moved from New York City to Taos, New Mexico, with the hope of accumulating more stories but not pacifying her ever-present wanderlust.*

JENNICA PETERSON

⋆ ✳ ⋆

The Miniature Mariachi Band Panties Invasion

There was a picnic in her pants.

I GRABBED MY CROTCH AS IF I WERE IN A MICHAEL JACKSON dance moves contest within thirty seconds of stepping out of the pouring rain and meeting the Paraguayan host family of my boyfriend's Peace Corps friend. This is not my normal behavior when I meet strangers, nor is it an ancient Paraguayan mating ritual. It's just that right as I met all eight of my hosts, plus their two curious neighbors, something bit me hard right where it counts.

I tried to be discreet at first, gently patting the painful spot while shaking hands and exchanging poorly pronounced formal Spanish greetings. My *"con mucho gusto"* came out like "¡*CON muCHO guSTO!*" as I grinned and rubbed away à la Madonna in one of her videos. The mother of the family began to smile like she'd just met a known international criminal, but didn't want to let on that she knew who I was until the police were close at hand. I caught her furtively glancing down at my crotch and then up again at her husband. I imagined she was thinking, "Please don't let this lady hurt my children."

There it was again, a bite of grand proportions. And another, this time on my butt. I slapped hard, but with a smile, hoping to kill the merciless little bastard and to look casual at the same time. It wasn't working. After a few seconds of having your rear attacked, you begin to lose touch with reality. Suddenly the primal part of your brain in charge of that area takes over. I hit again and again, harder and harder until the higher powers of Butt Land brought me to my senses. I knew I had to say something, but all that came out of my mouth was, "*Alguna cosa pica*," which I think means, "Something bites." I guess that got the point across because the entire crowd exclaimed, "¡*Ahhhhhh!*" The mother looked particularly relieved that I wasn't just exposing her daughters to my oversexed American ways. "¡*Hormigas!*" she exclaimed.

Time out.

Try to imagine what *"hormigas,"* sounded like to a frantic non-spanish-speaking butt-slapper like me. At that panicked moment, I went through a list of images for a potential match. An exotic type of bologna? No. A soccer team? It would have to be a small one, but I could hear the mininewscaster yell, "Gooooaaalll!" A group of guerrilla Spanish prostitutes? Probably not. Think pain. Scorpions? Venomous snakes? A ruthless miniature mariachi band?

My boyfriend saved me from further fruitless self-inquiry. "Ants," he said. "*Hormigas* means ants."

The mother of the family rushed me into the tiny bathroom. As soon as she closed the door, I heard the family erupt in laughter. I pulled off my pants faster than you can say, "Brad Pitt's lying naked in my bedroom," to find about fifty large ants streaming up and down my legs. A few held on as if auditioning for parts in *Titanic 2*, but I took great pleasure in ruining their Hollywood dreams.

When I emerged from the bathroom, the family laughed with me as they explained that on the way from the bus to the house, I must have stepped on an ant hole that was in a frenzy because of the rain. Just as the host mother handed me a cup of tea, I felt a little pinch on my inner thigh. Now knowing my worthy opponent well, I headed straight for the bathroom, where I served quick and sweet revenge.

Jennica Peterson's other animal encounters include bathing an elephant in Nepal, swimming with piranhas in Brazil, and being bit by a monkey in Guatemala. She lives in Oakland, California, and is an intern at Travelers' Tales.

* ✱ *

Confessions of a Food Smuggler

Her cups runneth over.

I WAS ALWAYS A FOODIE, BUT I BECAME A FOOD SMUGGLER because of guilt. Oh, and smuggling was also a family tradition.

But first let me tell you about the foodie part. My mother used to tell everyone that, as a kid, I did not eat a human breakfast. This statement came from a woman who consumed coffee, Pall Mall cigarettes, and *The New York Times* crossword puzzle for her morning meal.

She loved to explain how she put out a mini-buffet for her picky eater.

"She will eat leftover spaghetti or a cup of pea soup or cheese and crackers, but don't you dare put any cereal, eggs, or toast in front of her," she would cheerfully relate, to anyone who would listen.

While my contemporaries went steady at dinnertime with SpaghettiOs or fish sticks, I never knew what ethnic dish Mom was cooking up.

Certainly all her culinary creativity primed me for my later adventures in food, first as a restaurant cook and then as a food writer.

Adding to our culinary delights, once a year, my uncle, the priest, would visit us bringing goodies from French Canada: exotic blood sausages and Black Diamond cheddar cheese.

I'm not sure if it was legal for Uncle Arthur to bring sausages and cheese over the border, but in any case, the food was a welcome reminder of my mother's roots.

His visit always inspired Mom to tell stories about her smuggling "career" during Prohibition. No, Mom was not dodging Elliot Ness or highballing truckloads of booze into the very, very dry U.S.

What she did do, several times, was visit our relatives in Quebec, and return on the train wearing a big old mouton coat, which helped hide the two bottles of Canadian whisky she had tied around her waist.

The booze was not for my mother, who walked on the wild side with an occasional wine spritzer, but for my dear old granddad, who loved his whisky. Grandpa Darius was convinced that Prohibition was a personal insult to his health and well-being.

This idea came from a man who once cooked a turtle in tea, because in his thinking, tea was good and turtle was good, so why not combine them? This was probably the first fusion dish, leading eventually to abominations like kiwi pizza and my own corned beef *egg foo yung*.

When I finally got to go to France, I was excited beyond words. I knew all the good things to eat in the world lived there.

Arriving in Lyon, the province that has more three-starred Michelin chefs than any other, I found the restaurants from the most acclaimed three-star to the simplest *bouchon*, just amazing.

I walked around the city, visiting churches and department stores. Growing hungry for lunch, I went to a *bouchon*, the Lyon equivalent of a bistro.

I chowed down on blood sausages with apples, and eggy brioche bread with a schmear of the most heavenly paté.

I was having a great time, but to my disappointment (and guilt) my long-time boyfriend and fellow gourmand wasn't there to see and taste what I was experiencing.

The day before I was to return to San Francisco, I discovered Les Halles, the large public market of Lyon, where dozens of purveyors sell their products under one roof.

As I traversed the stalls and counters, looking at the displays of seafood, nuts, vegetables, cheeses, and more kinds of sausages than I thought could be invented, the plot to smuggle some tastes for my boyfriend hatched.

At the sausage emporium, I spoke to a young woman in broken French. I told her I was leaving the next day, and I wanted to bring some *saucisson* Lyonaise to my sweetheart.

After she translated my request to her mother, the older woman said in halting English, "I will take them to the factory and put them in plastic, so the dog does not smell them."

They told me to return the next day to pick them up. I was overjoyed with my purchase—about two pounds of cooked sausages—individually cryovaced.

> So there we were, five middle-aged women driving the streets of a small suburb of Fresno, looking for something we'd once loved and experienced only rarely in our adult lives. We were in search of a butterscotch-dipped ice cream cone and we weren't above accosting strangers to find it.
>
> ♦
>
> —Kathryn Pritchett,
> "Looking for Love in
> All the Wrong Places"

Arriving early at the market, I put them in my carry-on and took off for the airport. I couldn't wait to see his face, when Mr. Stay-At-Home sat down to some yummy sausages, good bread, and grainy mustard.

When I got to the airport, I started having trepidation about the sausages in my carry-on. That's when it hit me. I could stuff the sausages in my bra. I was already well-endowed, I'd just look more busty.

In the airport ladies' room, shoving in all the plastic sealed sausages wasn't easy. When I put my blazer back on, it protruded on both sides of my handsome full bosom. I was the Dolly Parton of Air France for sure.

No one can imagine how uncomfortable pieces of hard plastic are when they are digging into your soft flesh on a nine-hour flight. Nearing New York, the Air France steward handed me a declaration printed in French. I signed it: "No, I didn't have any *viande* (meat)."

If I got caught, I would plead ignorant of what it said.

At customs, my two pounds of sausages breezed through. In the airport ladies' room, I unloaded my cache.

Later that night, as my honey enjoyed his repast he said, "It's good to know I was in your thoughts and in your heart."

He never knew how close to my heart he (and his dinner) had been.

In years to come, I stuffed a black truffle in a potato chip container, a grapevine in my makeup case, and cheese in my packed underwear.

And if it weren't for that clever beagle at SFO, I would have had brie for all my pals. My smuggling career ended when the beagle sniffed at my bag and barked. I was busted. The customs officer said the food would be thrown away.

Defiantly, I sat on the edge of the luggage carousel and ate some of the cheese, straight with no bread or crackers.

My smuggling career was over and I had (*urp*) indigestion for days.

GraceAnn Walden has written a weekly column entitled the "Inside Scoop" for the San Francisco Chronicle *since 1991. She covers news about local chefs, new restaurants and issues within the food industry. Her new column, "Cooks Night Out," appears in the Chronicle's Pink Pages on Sundays. Her story, "Chocolate with Julia," was included in* Her Fork in the Road. *She conducts history-culinary tours of North Beach and Nob Hill in San Francisco on Saturdays. She lives in Marin with her gourmand Chihuahua, Cosmo, and her cat, Kinky.*

BRIGID KELSO

* ✷ *

Open Your Mouth and Say *Om*

It'll only hurt a little bit…

WOLFGANG PROUDLY RAISES HIS "NORTH FAKE" FLEECE ZIP-up. "This is where she bit me," he says nonchalantly, as our eyes fasten on the chain of purplish hickeys running counterclockwise from navel to kidneys along his six-pack abs.

"I mean sucked," he corrects himself.

Wolf's right. There are definitely teeth marks, but the skin hasn't been broken. The rest of us lift our jaws and bottles of Tuborg off the table. We want to order another round before Happy Hour ends at KC's Bar in Thamel, the touristy part of Kathmandu, where all the backpackers hang out.

Wolf had heard through the traveler grapevine about a mysterious Tibetan faith healer who could diagnose an illness by literally sucking the offending substance from a patient's body.

"What did she say was wrong with you?" asks Liz, another trekker.

"Too much hashish," he replies in clipped, Germanic syllables. "But she spat out kidney stones." Wolf goes on to tell us how the healer repeatedly hit him on the back of the head with a large, dull knife. He claims this was punishment for the hash, not the kidney blockage.

Liz figures she'll go see the healer for a laugh, if nothing else.

I, on the other hand, am more serious about this. I'd just returned from Tibet, where I'd watched hundreds of pilgrims circle Jokhang Temple in Lhasa, prostrating themselves in prayer for hours until filthy and sweating from this ritual they believe will ensure their entry to heaven. I admire these people for their tremendous faith.

We get the address of the famed healer, Llamo Dolkar, from Wolf and agree to meet in front of one of Thamel's many "German" Bakeries at 8:30 the next morning.

It's 8:35 and the fog (and pollution) is still thick in the valley as I gnaw on a day-old croissant in front of the just-opened bakery. There is no yeasty aroma of fresh-baked bread here. The bed-headed, bleary-eyed baker stumbles into the shop. The name, like all the other bakeries in town, says German, but like everything else here, it runs on Nepalese time—which means there's never a white-hatted employee rushing in at 4 A.M., sliding trays of rising, doughy orbs into the oven. With the country's itinerant electricity, they'd probably turn into pitas anyway.

Liz approaches from the direction exactly opposite her hotel, in exactly the same midriff-baring, hip-hugging outfit she had on the night before. Also hugging her is a hip Israeli with long, shampoo-ad tresses, pushed back with a plastic tortoiseshell hair band—Liz's. He returns the hair band to its owner's unwashed head and kisses it.

Then, hands in pockets, he saunters off, whistling, perhaps in search of another hair ornament and girl to go with it.

"I was very bad last night," Liz giggles.

"Are you sure you want to do this today?" I ask, imagining she must be exhausted, hung over, and wanting a change of clothes. Perhaps not really the best shape to be whacked repeatedly on the head with a large knife.

I remind her that we're going to see a spiritual person—the equivalent of confessing to a priest with X-ray vision into your soul, or Santa Claus: he knows if you've been bad or good, etc. But Liz is still up for it.

A rickshaw driver drops us across from Nepal's second favorite postcard—the Bodhanath—the famed white-domed monolith, whose heavy-lidded Buddha eyes survey the entire Himalayan-ringed Kathmandu Valley. Below, perspiring pilgrims circumambulate the temple, spinning prayer wheels. One corner is a religious mini-gym, where the more cardio-keen prostrate themselves with such fervor, you'd swear they were getting paid for each full-body genuflection. In North America, they would be. I can see it now—the donations would go to prostate cancer, and everyone would get a t-shirt.

Our driver watches us march self-confidently down an alley where flea-ridden stray dogs copulate or root through garbage heaps as high as fences on either side.

At the back of the building on the left is a puddle of excrement, human or animal, we're not sure. Llamo can't be doing much business living in the likes of this place, I think.

Still, we climb three flights of stairs, where we are welcomed by several signs: "This is not a freak show." "Only those who believe will be healed." "Sorry, no women during their period; you're welcome to come back when you're clean."

Llamo's husband, Tenba, greets us at the door, which is open and covered, Tibetan-style, with a curtain. He speaks a little English, asks where we're from, and hands us glasses of hot, sweet tea. We each give him US$5 and sit cross-legged on cushions on the floor in the "living-room." Beside us is a Western couple probably in their late thirties, eyes closed and chanting as they finger the wooden prayer beads on their wrists and around their necks. There is also a Hindu family—mom, dad, and their teenaged son. I wonder out loud to Liz what everyone is here to be cured of.

In the corner is a small altar with a photo of the Dalai Lama, brightly-colored silk scarves, and many brass items, including five little lamps holding yak butter and several serious-looking dagger-type knives or small swords (all of which I imagine coming down with brute force upon my noggin). There is also what looks like a putty knife, a bell, several bowls containing lumps of yak butter and milk, and a spoon. On the floor, next to the altar, is a green bowl filled with *tsampa* (a barley and butter mixture eaten mainly by monks), an empty bowl, a little drum, and a full-length striped apron-tunic typically worn by Tibetan women.

After the money is collected, Llamo Dolkar enters the room. She's in her late fifties, and about five-foot-eight—tall for a woman in this part of the world. Her waist-length, graying hair hangs in a ponytail down her back. She sits quietly, meditating I guess, then washes her hands in one of the bowls and rinses out her mouth. Her husband then sprinkles water on her, the room, and us.

Llamo stands on a mat facing the altar, breathes deeply, stretches her arms in front of her, closes her eyes, yawns loudly and brings her hands together, over her head, touching them to her forehead and her chest—the first two gestures of the pilgrims' prostration. She chants a mantra in a low monotone.

Suddenly, her arms wing out, she makes three full prostrations before the altar, and her body begins to tremble. She yells what I think is "f—k" three times (or maybe it's me, so freaked out by the she-devil psyching herself up), lets out a loud shriek, then cackles like a witch. Llamo is now possessed by her goddess who gives her the power to heal. She murmurs, laughs, then hiccups.

I notice the open window. What will the neighbors think? But the Third World cacophony of horns honking, dogs barking, and children yelling in the street is more a distraction to us than Llamo is to it.

For years, people thought Dolkar, a Tibetan refugee, was insane. As a teen, she moved to a convent, where she endured sudden outbursts and tremendous pain, as it's told, because the goddess was trying to possess her. Dolkar had dreams that led her to wander around India, from Delhi to Ladakh to Calcutta, healing people. She had trouble keeping jobs, but luckily, her husband eventually believed that his wife had special powers, and he worked to support the two of them and their son.

One day, the healer was fortunate enough to meet her guru, who told her what she had to do in order for the goddess to enter her. But it wasn't until she was into her forties that she became recognized by the Dalai Lama as housing the special powers of the goddess, Dorje Yudronma, and given the title, "Llamo," meaning goddess. She does not permit photos or interviews.

Llamo is breathless. She sits, legs folded, in front of us, ties the tunic around her waist and fits a red cloth scullcap on her head. She holds the bell and spoon in her left hand and the drum in her right. While ringing the bell and hitting the drum, she flings barley and liquid butter all over the altar and upon anyone who is near. She spoons a little milk into the bowl on the floor. After chanting for about five minutes, she starts a fast, high-pitched song, moving her head, trance-like, from side to side. This lasts a couple of minutes. Tenpa, meanwhile, cleans up the mess his wife has made with small squares of toilet paper. Llamo puts down her instruments, covers her lap with a cloth and faces us. She's now ready for her first vict…I mean patient.

The man with the beads is first. Tenba (Llamo speaks less English than he does) asks him what's wrong.

"My back," he answers. Llamo chants something, then gets Tenba to help her turn the man around and hold him down. He winces while Llamo sucks something out of his back and spits it into the empty brass bowl beside them. His significant other has her eyes closed and is frantically fingering those wooden beads and whispering. Liz raises her eyebrows, shrugs, and gives me that "it's a piece of cake" look. The man, who now has a big, red welt on his back, re-buttons his shirt and returns to his cushion on the floor.

His partner is next. This one's a no-brainer for Llamo. After looking briefly at her face, Llamo diagnoses (through Tenpa) that the woman has acne and should buy some Dettol anti-bacterial soap to get rid of it.

Now the Hindu couple bring their son forward. Llamo discusses the problem with them in Hindi. They respond in words and head wagging that I'm sure must translate into "We're at our wits' end. We've tried everything we can, but he just won't listen."

The son hangs his head in shame as they leave him at the altar.

Llamo grabs one of the small swords and whacks the kid on the head, neck, shoulders, and down his back. She yells at the lad what I imagine is "take that," and "if I *ever* catch you doing *that* again…" The youth whimpers, head still down. Liz's eyes bug out, she furrows her brow, and her body quivers empathetically with each blow he gets.

"Maybe his parents caught him doing drugs," she whispers into my ear.

"Or spanking the monkey," I whisper back.

The healer finishes her treatment by splashing water all over the boy's head and down his shirt. She tells him to go. His parents grab him by the scruff of the neck, stuff some rupee notes into Tenpa's hand, then back out of the room, almost doubling over in gratitude before Llamo.

Tenpa, smiling, asks which of us is next. Liz is shaking. Dehydration, a high blood-alcohol level, and guilt from the night

I've never been one to take the safe route, live the sheltered life. When we were in London doing our semester abroad, my pal Sam and I used to make fun of our classmates who donned their red Reeboks and boarded huge, insulated coach buses to go see the sights. We pointed and laughed at them up there in their cushy seats, then we'd strap on backpacks and do things the way the locals would.

◆

—Suz Redfearn,
"Fantasy Island"

before have culminated in a punishment she knows will only worsen over the next few minutes.

"I want to get it over with before I throw up," she says, offering to go before me. Liz holds onto my hand tightly. She explains the problem to Tenba, who, I might add, seems just a tad too eager to lift her shirt. ("Lucky I was wearing my good bra," she later confided to me.) Llamo takes one look at the silver hoop in Liz's navel and asks out loud in perfect English, "Why?" Careful to avoid the pierced belly-button, she leans into her patient's stomach. Liz squeezes my hand even harder, letting up only after the possessed one's chops have left her flesh.

Finished, Liz trades places with me—grinning like a kid who's made her First Confession, and gets off with just one Our Father and a couple Glory Be's.

I'm next. Llamo fingers a vein on my wrist, and runs her other hand up and down my thin, trembling arms. Then she looks right into my eyes and tells me her diagnosis. In the five seconds it takes her husband to translate, I am convinced I have cancer. I am dead. I picture the Embassy calling my parents, the coffin being shipped back to Canada—but what coffin? Corpses are set on fire in Hindu countries. Then Tenba states: "Your left side is colder than your right side. The circulation is bad."

Llamo gently tilts my head down, and I silently thank the powers that be for my life, promising to do only good work from now on, when it hits me. First I receive the blow to the back of my neck, then repeatedly down the entire left side of my body with what I hope is only the putty knife.

Tenba raises my t-shirt and his wife takes six soft bites of my arms, shoulder and back. After the ceremony, Tenba scribbles a prescription, illegible in any language, on a scrap of paper, and attempts to direct Liz and me through the town's medieval, labyrinthine alleyways to a Tibetan drug store.

The pharmacist's shelves are lined with glass jars holding hundreds of brown, woody balls—some small as pearls—others big as jaw-breakers. I pay about fifty cents for a two-centimeter sphere, wrapped in a tiny red cloth, nestled in a small, clear plastic box. Directions in English are included on a bubble-gum-like wrapper folded up inside.

"Pinchen Mangjor Chnmo (The Great Precious Accumulation Pill)" is made of about fifty ingredients, including gold, silver, iron, coral, and turquoise. It's supposed to pacify "404 ailments caused by disorders of blood." It should not be exposed to bright light, but must be taken in dim light only. Preparations involve soaking it in boiling water overnight, then breaking it up into another cup of hot water. It should then be covered with a clean cloth and allowed to stand overnight. The next morning I must recite the mantra, *"Tadyatha aum bhaishjaya maha bhaishjya raja samud Ga-te Svaha,"* (but I fear I'll mispronounce one of the syllables and accidentally turn a friend into a donkey like Samantha did on *Bewitched*), then stir the mixture and drink it. "Follow with another cup of hot water," say the directions, "and go to bed with warm clothes."

For the next two days, I have to avoid meat, eggs, garlic, raw veggies, raw grain (darn), fried foods, sexual intercourse, and cold baths. "Except in cases of emergency, the pill must be taken only on such auspicious days as a full or new moon."

On the way back to our guesthouse, Liz and I go into hysterics as we invent ailments and how Llamo would treat those afflicted. I ask her what she would do if the guy she slept with the night before showed up on Llamo's doorstep with V.D. We have to stop the rickshaw so Liz can vomit on the side of the road.

A few days later, I move on to India, where the remedy slides to the bottom of my backpack, and, after a few weeks, I forget about the whole thing.

Back in Canada, I tell few friends about my experience with Llamo Dolkar. I get the feeling people think I'm making it up.

Every Christmas, I buy a multicultural calendar from a Toronto artist, who uses themes, such as color, peace, or the family, in her paintings. This year's theme is creation myths from around the world. I flip to November, where my eyes fix on the image of a woman who looks as if she's being possessed. The caption below reads, "Tibetan Healer goes into trance."

"That reminds me of someone I once met," I say.

"That's my friend in Nepal—Llamo Dolkar," says the artist, a beautiful, South Asian woman. The calendar slides from my hands and back onto the table.

"We need to talk," I tell her.

Brigid Kelso has been discouraged from writing all her life. After two years as a correspondent for a farm weekly, her editor suggested that she try teaching. A month after quitting the paper, she won a Canadian writer's award. Just before this story was published, she was told by a prize-winning author that her humor "just doesn't translate to the page." She now takes advice from nobody. In addition to editing an online publication and teaching business English to non-native speakers in Toronto, she travels around the globe, having stayed with locals in two dozen countries and attempting thirteen languages. She also writes stories for the Globe and Mail *and* Outpost *magazine, and photographs cats for calendars. Brigid has stayed with locals in almost two dozen countries and attempted 13 languages. Although she once photographed the same Borneo Penan tribeswoman as did famed anthropologist, Wade Davis, it was his which appeared in* National Geographic. *He has since been informed that she took hers first.*

LIZ SCOTT

* ✳ *

Entomology and Earplugs

A holiday at the Roach Motel.

EVERY TIME I TRAVEL SOMEPLACE I FORGET TO PACK SOME-thing. For my honeymoon, I forgot my earplugs. No big deal, I figured—there's not much need for earplugs on a beautiful uncrowded island in French Polynesia. I was wrong about that, though not for any reason I might have anticipated.

My husband and I honeymooned on the lovely small island of Moorea, with verdant valleys and crystal blue lagoons, far more primitive than the Hawaiian Islands most Americans visit. There are no high-rise condominiums or giant American resort hotel complexes. Instead, little individual grass-roofed bungalow rooms surround larger low buildings housing the restaurants, bars, and shops. Almost everything is open air with screens and open spaces instead of doors and windows.

Our charming just-off-the-beach bungalow was not one of the fancy ones. We had screens but no glass in our win-dows, and the occasional beetle crawling across the floor. It seemed charming to us until our third night. That balmy Friday evening found us in bed early. I was recovering from a cold, and we were both still feeling some jet lag. So by nine P.M. we were drifting off to sleep.

Suddenly, something was scrabbling at my left ear. In my near-unconscious state, I tried to remove the something by jabbing a finger at it. In hindsight, what I actually did was poke an insect that was halfway there all the way down into my ear canal.

I leapt out of bed screaming. My darling husband of a whopping five days, who had been asleep, sat up and groggily inquired what on earth was the matter with me.

"Get it out get it out get it out!!!" I shrieked.

"Get what out?" he asked.

"There's a bug in my ear. Get it out!" I screamed.

At that point, my husband came to the sleep-fogged but not unreasonable conclusion that a mosquito had flown into my ear and for some reason I was hysterical about it. He suggested I pour a little water into my ear and let it drain back out, in order to flush out the "mosquito." I loudly explained that his suggestion would not work. I was too panicky and incoherent to express that the insect in my ear was very large, hard-shelled, alive, and trying desperately to escape the small space into which it was wedged by scrabbling with little sharp-clawed feet. Part of the problem was that I'd managed to shove the little beast in deep enough to be invisible outside my ear. My husband couldn't see anything wrong.

Eventually we made it to the bathroom, where to humor my husband I tried the water trick. Unsurprisingly, it didn't work. My husband, who was still trying to wake up, asked repeatedly if we could please deal with this tomorrow. I repeatedly replied that NO, we could NOT deal with this tomorrow. There was no way I could lie back down and sleep like this.

After about fifteen minutes of screaming and jumping up and down, a sort of calm settled over me. The panic abated as I came to the conclusion that nothing could be done about the bug immediately. I'd also managed to figure out that opening my mouth to scream was making my ear hurt more.

I asked my husband if we had tweezers. We both searched and came up empty-handed, so I suggested that we go up to the front desk and see if they had any. He agreed.

On the way down the fragrant path to the front desk, the humor in the situation struck me. I realized that I was going to have to explain to a hotel desk clerk, in French, "Help! I have a big bug in my ear." This thought inspired a feeble round of giggling, which greatly cheered my poor husband. Upon reaching the front desk, I was grateful to find that the woman on duty spoke English. I explained the situation to her and requested a pair of tweezers. Despite a significant level of distraction, I did notice the number of hotel employees staring at me in wonder as the clerk explained to them in French what was going on and went off in search of the requested implement.

She returned with tweezers and flashlight, took a quick look in my ear with the flashlight, and saw nothing. She looked at me, looked at the tweezers, and realized that she could not stick a sharp implement into the ear of a hotel guest. So she handed the tools over to my husband. He took a look for himself, and initially saw nothing but darkness with a couple of light lines. Then he realized with horror that what he was looking at was not my empty ear—it was the back end of a large black insect completely filling my ear canal. He stopped mumbling "can we deal with this tomorrow" and started saying "hospital please."

The desk clerk heard him and more importantly saw the look on his face, and dialed the hospital. At this point, we hit a limitation of our unspoiled tropical island. There were no taxis that operated at night. There were no buses or shuttles after sunset. No rental car agencies stayed open past five P.M. The clerk assisting us didn't own a car herself—a not uncommon circumstance on the island. We couldn't even rent a bicycle. It was ten P.M. and the hospital was five miles away. I was in no condition to walk that far. Yet this didn't really seem like an emergency warranting an ambulance. So how were we going to get me to and from the hospital?

The answer came in the form of an employee of the hotel bar who did own a car. She'd just finished her shift and was headed home, so we decided to deal with the issue of how we'd get back from the hospital to the hotel later. So my husband and I crammed into the tiny LeCar knockoff with the cocktail waitress and the two co-workers she was also taking home. As the injured party, I got the front seat. The three women in the car spoke almost no English and my husband spoke no French, so I endeavored to chat with them and act as translator, all with my head tilted to one side and the occasional whimper when the bug made another attempt to gain its freedom with its scratchy little claws. I am functional in French, but not fluent. All three women were quite concerned about me, and I was able to convey that yes, it hurt a great deal but I was sure it would all be O.K.

We arrived at the tiny island hospital and two nurses whisked me off to what passed as the emergency room. The three women from the hotel chose to stay and wait with my husband so they could drive us back to the hotel, bless them.

Apparently this sort of thing does not happen often in French Polynesia, despite it being a tropical, and hence, bug-ridden place. If I'd stepped on a poisonous rock fish, as happened to another guest at our hotel, they would have known exactly what to do and I would have been in and out in less than ten minutes. If it had been in New York, where I later learned that such incidents are commonplace and the tools to deal with them are standard in emergency rooms, I would have been in and out in less than ten minutes.

As it was, I spent forty-five minutes in the emergency room, undergoing attempted bug-removal procedures I will endeavor not to dwell upon. However, it's worth noting that when a bug of this type is broken in half and pieces of it are yanked away, it does not die. It panics, and attempts to run. This is unpleasant if it is trying to run deeper into one's ear. Happily, I also learned that a half-dismembered panicking bug can be killed by attempting to flush it from the ear with a stream of water. The flushing procedure does not, mind you, remove the bug from the ear. But the bug's death by drowning *does* stop it from further wriggling around and clawing at the ear, which is a relief to the owner of the ear.

Finally, after listening to forty minutes of agonized moaning and crying from me, the nurses gave up and fetched a doctor. The doctor shambled in—he'd obviously been dragged from a comfortable bed to treat me. He asked for something in French that sounded like "forceps." The nurses searched but could not produce it, so he had a try with the vacuum machine the nurses had already tried. For obvious reasons, they could not use a high level of suction with this machine—bursting my eardrum would not have helped remove the insect. The attempt failed, so he proceeded to rifle the shelves and drawers for the forceps himself. He found them, inserted them into my ear, removed what was left of the bug, glared at the nurses as if to say "you woke me up for *this*?" and shambled back out.

On his way back to bed, he passed my husband and the three women from the hotel. Despite the language barrier, my husband and the women found ways to communicate and had a grand time trying to chat in the waiting area. The women stopped the doctor to ask how things had gone. He assured them that I was just fine now. Though my husband did not understand their words, it became evident that one of the women had asked him how big the bug was. The doctor, with a deadpan expression on his face, looked down and spanned his hands about two feet apart. The women stared in shock while my husband, who quickly figured out the gist of the exchange, began laughing out loud. The doctor went back to bed.

Though I was still in pain, relief overwhelmed me. One of the nurses cleaned out my ear with some sort of antiseptic solution, and they gave me a short form to fill out. I fully expected to pay for the services and had even remembered to bring my wallet, but they never asked for any money. Socialized medicine is a grand thing. I asked what kind of bug it was, and they said it was "*un cafre*." I decided to figure out what that meant the next day, and assumed it was one of the black beetles we'd seen in our room earlier in the week.

We all piled back into the subcompact car and headed for the hotel. Now that I was debugged, the women felt they could chat more openly with me and became incredibly friendly. They wanted to take us up to see a pretty view of the hotel from a cliff. They wanted to know where we came from. They wanted to know if the singer Cher was a woman or a man—apparently a point of hot debate since the release of "Do You Believe" on the island radio stations.

The view was lovely, and the woman from the bar told us a beautiful Tahitian legend about one of the Southern constellations. Finally, we returned to the hotel and to our bungalow. Sleep was sweet, particularly after I found a suitable piece of cloth to tie about around my head, covering my ears. I continued this practice for the rest of our honeymoon.

The next morning, I went down to the desk to let the woman who'd helped us know that everything turned out all right. She expressed her happiness and relief, and offered us a nicer bungalow for the duration of our visit—one directly on the beach with glass windows and fewer insects. We accepted. When we moved in, a free bottle of champagne sat cooling in an ice bucket for us.

I asked what "*un cafre*" was, and was told it was a roach. I got the heebies all over again knowing that. Somehow a beetle had seemed less repulsive than a roach.

That night at the hotel restaurant, we gave our name and were unexpectedly escorted to front row seats in the restaurant for the dinner show. Somehow, we always got good seats for the shows after that. Before dinner that night we'd gone to the oceanfront bar and had drink after drink pressed on us by our new friend, the waitress with the car. Over the next ten days, we imbibed upwards of $300 in free drinks, all courtesy of my "*cafre.*" All we had to do was ignore the glances and titters of the hotel staff every time we gave our name. We had become famous throughout the establishment, even to the staff members who had never seen us before.

Were the drinks and the good seats and the nicer room worth it? Quite frankly, no. Next time I'll happily pay for my Planter's Punch if it means my ears stay roach-free. But I realized, even that fateful night when the blasted critter was still in my ear, that I had a choice. The Unfortunate Roach Incident could ruin my honeymoon, or it could become a great story. I love a great story. My husband and I are even thinking of returning to Moorea for our tenth wedding anniversary. I'm sure I'll remember earplugs that time.

Liz Scott was raised in the San Francisco Bay Area. In 1996 she graduated from Stanford University with a degree in English and a hope that she wouldn't be making a career out of the phrase "Do you want fries with that?" She now works in Silicon Valley as a technical writer. Her husband decided to stick with her since she was such a good sport about the honeymoon; they have been married for two and a half years and still enjoy traveling together. When she's not traveling, she enjoys cooking, reading, motorcycling, and medieval sword fighting.

✳

When I called my best friend the day we left and told her I'd started my period the night before our camping trip in the Ozarks, she said, very emphatically, "OHMYGOD, the bears are going to get you."

She didn't say, "OHMYGOD. There are bloodsucking ticks in the woods. You'll attract ticks to you like bears to honey."

I hung up the phone and checked my trusty outdoors resource about menstruating women, and it said I had nothing to worry about. As far as bears were concerned.

I woke in the middle of the night, slithering in insect repellant, and was startled at two, looming eyes a hair's breadth away, just outside the mesh tent wall. It was Penny still sitting up, still staring inside the tent. I gave in and let her curl up at my feet. She immediately flopped on her back, all four legs stick-straight in the air.

I felt a tickle on my skin. It was a tick on my stomach, heading south, of course. I found another crawling on the outside of my underwear—it was too hot to wear pajamas. What was it? Had we pitched our tent in a bed of ticks? Had we discovered their lair? Their secret mating grounds? Was this the womb of tickdom? The crack in the earth where all the ticks in the world received their marching orders? The very center of tick civilization?

As I closed my eyes, I felt a tick crawling in another place, thank God not my crotch. This time in my ear. I reached in with my fingertip but didn't feel anything. It crept deeper, nesting in the depths of my ear, inside my head, gorging and growing heavy with my life supply as the night ticked on. In the morning, I had Eric look inside. He found a dog hair.

—Kim Steutermann Rogers, "Tick. Tick. Tick."

* * *

Pleasure Tips

Who could have known it would feel so good?

BECAUSE I LIVE ALONE WITH A CAT, MY GREATEST MOMENTS of sensual pleasure since living and teaching in China have come from having someone diddling around in my ears with a Q-tip. I think the whole experience at the "hair shop" is the most surprising experience, and the best bargain in China. It is an opportunity to close my eyes for most of an hour, yield myself up to others' hands and to feel like a queen. A spoiled and indulged queen. A queen who moans.

Recently the textbook for my English classes had a unit of health called "Grandma Knows Best." It was on traditional remedies around the world, the kind of remedies that "Grandma" knows. So I began the class asking everyone to tell the group what they would do for themselves if they had a headache. Many of the students said they would go to the hair shop for hair washing. Me too. It works.

The first time I had this treatment, in Ningbo, I thought I was just going to the barber's for a haircut. Of course it would be washed, too. A Chinese friend took me there and asked if

I would like a massage of my head and shoulders, too. I asked what it would cost. All of it, wash, cut, massage would be about $2.50. Less than a gin and tonic. I thought I would be out of there in less than half an hour.

The young girl sat me in a chair (the only one in the place) put a big splat of cheap shampoo in her hand, smeared it around on the crown of my head, added a squirt of water and started rubbing it around, lathering it up. And then she rubbed it around and around, here and there on my head using a variety of finger maneuvers. She seemed to be thoroughly rubbing every follicle and centimeter of my scalp. I stole a look at my watch. Ten minutes. When was she going to rinse me? She scraped all the suds off so I thought rinsing was imminent, but no, she added another splash of water and whipped up a fresh array of snowy mountain peaks on my head using her repertoire of strokes, flicks, scratches, tugs, and rubs. She also rubbed my neck, temples, forehead, and shoulders. That was when I decided to stop checking my watch for some time warp of a mistake until the end. It lasted a full hour before the haircut. And there was no misunderstanding about money as I had feared. It was that cheap.

Since then I have had many, many hair washes in China, with no haircut. In Xiamen, they cost less than $1.50, less than a cup of coffee. They last about an hour. Someone rubs your scalp, neck, shoulders, back, and arms in an infinite array of strokes that have all been taught by some official organization because there is a basic set (like they all make little tiny squeezes all along the outer edges of the ears several times) with some variations, just a little individuality.

And some room for genius. The people who do this are the lowest of the lowly employees in the beauty salons and hair shops (men and women go to both), where they are not

allowed to cut or comb or style hair, only massage and shampoo. I have found two of these young people who have miracle hands, doing the kind of massage we pay $40–60 an
hour for in America. Healer's hands. And for each of them,
after the first "hair washing" I dug into my little pocket dictionary and found the characters for "medicine" and "hands."
They each understood and grinned and blushed and bowed.
But I bowed lower. They were healers.

It was one of these medicine-hand people, a woman about
thirty, who first stuck a Q-tip in my ear. All the hair washers
before had handed me a few Q-tips and I dried in there all
by myself. But she snuck up on me with the Q-tip. I was surprised, felt a little invaded, slightly alarmed, but managed to
relax. It felt wonderful. When she began on the second ear I
had a picture in my head of my old dog from my childhood,
a dog whose impeccable dignity could only be ruffled by one
thing—rubbing his ears. He would moan. He would drool,
seeming to lose control of his lips. I kept as much control as
you must being a stranger in a strange country. I think I did
moan just a little.

Today I was in the barber's in my little neighborhood. I
was hoping that the boy who couldn't be past nineteen, who
has washed my hair and rubbed me all those other places
many times while I sat in his chair, would be there. But it was
Sunday and he was not. Lots of men sitting around smoking
and talking loudly over the blaring TV no one was watching.
No one was having anything done to their hair. I thought
maybe it was a closed-for-business day. But a young woman
in a very short, pale-pink dress and extremely high, hot-pink
platform shoes appeared through the cigarette haze. She
looked like an angel who had gotten past the fashion police
and then she made that beautiful Oriental gesture of open

reception with her hand, the gesture that led me to a chair.

At first I thought that the whole experience was going to be shot down by all the noise. Everything the Chinese do is LOUD. I am used to that, but the TV today was alive with gunshots and other sounds of violence and the group of men were all talking louder than that and the pink angel who had her hands in my hair was also unabashedly watching the tube. I just closed my eyes like I always do. I am at that age where there is little pleasure in sitting in front of a mirror in a well-lit room for an hour.

I was grumbly at first, meditating on the "fatal flaw" in nearly all Chinese experiences. The sublime touching that goes on in the barber's is always held in check from complete bliss meltdown by the noise in those places. But

—— ☽ ——

While stuck in traffic, the taxi driver rolled up a sleeve, rubbed his baby-butt smooth arm, and grinned: "*Wo mei you maoer!*" I have no hair!

I rolled up my sleeve and twisted a patch of Chicana-black arm hairs. "*Wo you!*" I have some!

Then he lifted his pant leg to expose a second hairless limb.

Not having shaved in months, I had an impressive collection in store.

"*Aiya!*" he cringed, then looked away.

We sat in silence for the rest of the trip. I assumed my gorilla-girl legs had been a major turn-off, but he slipped me a piece of paper as I climbed out of his cab. A phone number was scribbled across it. As I looked up in surprise, he blew me a kiss before roaring away.

◆

—Stephanie Elizondo Griest,
Around the Bloc

the girl in the pink angel outfit wrangled all the grumpiness right out of my head in just a few moments. She knew where it hurt. She knew where the grumble-loops were. Her fingers knew where to go to make the dragons scram out of their stinky little caves under my shoulder blades. She rubbed my temples in firm circles until they were as smooth, calm, and full of serenity as lily ponds. She did little things with her fingernails all along my eyebrows that no one has ever done before. I was putty, Silly Putty. I could not stop smiling with my eyes closed, something like the Buddha trying not to crack up.

And then she rinsed me. This rinsing is always one of the very best parts of the whole event. Lying back with my head cradled in the black basin as unconscious and thought-free as if I had been beheaded while still smiling. They choose the right temperature for the day and my mood, they lift my head, turn it slightly for proper run off, slide their snaky little fingers all through it. And then they slide a finger into the ear canal to block it while rinsing the outer ears. There is a slight quality of bodily invasion each time, but, oh, oh, it feels so good. So intimate. I think maybe the pink girl today knew I felt a lot of pleasure about that. She did it three times. I think I lost consciousness for a few seconds there. *Petite mort.*

She spent at least three times longer than anyone ever has rinsing my hair. She wiped my neck and forehead several times with a hot washcloth. I wanted to lick her hand a few times. I was limp when she raised me up toward my feet again. That old posture where I must carry my head around on top of my body. It really wasn't my first choice right then. But I did walk back to the chair and submit to hair rubbing with some gratuitous shoulder squeezing tossed in again. Then she snuck up on me with the Q-tip. I felt it start to slide in my ear canal like a very familiar animal, something like a domesticated and affectionate pussy willow bloom. I just closed my eyes. I did not feel invaded this time. I had more than an inkling of what this girl could do to me.

She did that. And more. Finally, I was glad for all the noise in the shop. I did moan. I consciously tried not to do my version of the "I want what she ordered" scene in the restaurant from "Harry Meets Sally," because that belongs to Meg Ryan for all time. But, if people could have heard me over the din, they would have all wanted it with a Q-tip then and there, too.

She combed me. I waved away the blow dryer. She flicked my hair into the right places with her fingers. She patted my little head to show she was pleased with how it looked. I nodded like the mute I had become, still agog from how it all felt beneath my hair and up my ear canals. I paid the little bit of money, and I knew better than to try to tip. I squeezed her hands, but did not kiss them. I might have lost control of my lips and drooled.

Karin Faulkner has been writing creatively her whole life, eventually working as a professional writer and creative writing teacher in California. In 1998 she cast off from the USA and went overseas to live in Asia, first in Indonesia and then to China. She believes that the most necessary thing for living in Asia is your sense of humor. You also must learn to appreciate ridiculous moments centering on your self. She usually finds the best way to handle the need to get something really important accomplished in Asia is to treat the desire as a brief illness, take two Extra Strength Tylenol, and go to bed with a good book.

* ✱ *

Aurora Borealis
and the Big Boom

Was it the song of the desert?

Sipping Jack Daniels and water, we trace the trajectory of Orion's belt as it wends its way across the deepening Kaibab sky. It's the end of a nine-day service trip to the Grand Canyon's North Rim and the six other campers have gone to bed, leaving Steve the chef, Theresa from Boston, and me as the designated wrapper-uppers. Our conversation runs the gamut of Bing vs. Sinatra to "Now the string theory is *what* again?"

As I see it, there are two sure-fire paths to lively conversation on a backpacking trip. One way to go is small. Offer up some of your dumbest observations. Discuss constitutionals. Imitate your cat yarking up a fur ball. Demonstrate your encyclopedic knowledge of Bugs Bunny or Monty Python routines. Try to uncover what, exactly, makes Adam Sandler a star.

The other way to go is big. Ask theoretical questions that have plagued mankind over the ages: Do we really only perceive things through metaphors? *Is* chaos the natural order of the universe? Raise your own theories about going home again. Chew the philosophical fat as you drink your nightcap. When the rationale has deteriorated to the "can so" "can't neither" stage, know enough to go to bed.

The three of us are getting all big right now, discussing travel and how our journeys have broadened and deepened our perspectives. Or at least we're trying. It's getting pretty late.

Suddenly, during Theresa's discourse on an experience she had in Alaska, we hear it: a curious noise, like medium-sized rocks tumbling down a steep cliff. Chatter ceases, it happens again: sharp, piff-like sounds coming from the little plateau above the escarpment where trip leader Tim had bunkered down.

Theresa starts, a bit spooked. "What was that?"

"Rocks or something," Steve replies. "So go on."

"Oh. O.K. Well anyway, the aurora borealis just blew my mind."

"ffffFFFFffftp!" Theresa cocks an ear just as a couple more small rounds erupt from the direction of trip leader Tim's sleeping silhouette. It takes a Grand Canyon minute but one by one, we get it.

Tim has gas.

Oh. Well then.

Theresa soldiers on as if she always hears farts that sound like sniper fire. "So the Eskimos had all these beliefs about the aurora, see. Some thought they were hunter spirits with lanterns looking for game, or ghosts playing a kind of soccer with walrus skulls."

"You don't say."

"Yup. Victorians thought the light was caused by icebergs crashing together in the sea."

"Hmm."

We lie back, silently contemplating walrus skulls, iceberg sparks, and what the hell is in Tim's diet. Finally Theresa breaks the silence, exposing the elephant in the outback. "Now should we debrief about the fart?"

I start to giggle. Steve, exacting chef type that he is, needs a little more clarification. "Should we wha…?"

"The fart. We all heard it," she says matter-of-factly. "We heard it, we took note of it, and we kept on with our conversation as if nothing had happened. I think we need to debrief about the fart."

Not only has Theresa left us with no choice, I think debriefing about the fart is a smashing idea. "God yes," I enthuse, "talk to me."

"Well I'm just saying, that was some fart." Theresa marvels.

"I can't believe he didn't wake himself up," Steve muses, truly impressed.

"I wonder if that happens at home. His poor wife," I offer.

"Yeah, that'd get old in a hurry," Theresa agrees. "Geez, it sounded like a machine gun."

"Now you're just being silly," Steve replies.

"Yeah," I add. "It was more like just a BB gun." After a short debate, we reach a consensus: it was, in fact, in the neighborhood of a BB gun.

Canyon silence returns.

"A very *big* BB gun though," Theresa concludes.

When small matters have been pondered and all big things have been made clear, when stars dance their slow waltz right on your head and whiskey shared tastes a little like the arc of falling leaves, when you can agree on the magnitude of someone else's flatulence, well, then, you know you're friends, and between big thoughts and the big boom, it's time to go to bed.

Inspired by Carol Burnett, Judy Zimola has wanted to be a comedian since she was seven. To that end, she tried musical theater, singing telegrams, and what she thought were amusing presentations at her company staff meetings. She has published articles in Fiddler *and* Nebraska Life *magazines and is now a freelance production artist and writer. She lives in Fairfax, California, and hikes in the Southwest whenever she can.*

Index of Contributors

Acknowledgments

The making of this book was a lot like a painting party. They did the work, and I'm writing up this page in lieu of the pizza and beer. I am truly humbled by the friends and family and second families that contributed immeasurable amounts of support, both emotional and financial, to me during the time I worked on this book.

As always, my kindred spirits at Travelers' Tales are at the core of this effort from beginning to end. Heartfelt mega-thanks to James O'Reilly for his positive foresight, unfailing belief in my potential on and off the book projects, and for calling me Little Sister at all the right times. Susan, I only want to repay your countless hours of work and devotion with multi-annual cocktail-induced vacation breaks. Many thanks to Sean O'Reilly for keeping my morality in check, as well as his tireless research efforts. For Krista, a shopping spree for all the clothes I've taken. All authors should be so fortunate to have their publicists be their friend first, and their namebuilder second. Many thanks to our interns for their enthusiastic and thoughtful work on this book: Cindy Williams, Alexandria Brady, Jennica Peterson, Eva Kent, and Christy Harrington. And finally a gigantic running-up hug to Larry Habegger, as much for your time on the book, as for your greater role in my life. You raise the bar for me Larry, and I continue to try to be a better person because of it.

To my entire herd of blood relatives: The Leos, Livingstons, and offshoots of both. Especially my dad, for his unconditional love.

And now I'd like to thank my global support system. The men of BootsnAll—Sean Keener, Chris Heidrich, Nick O'Neill: Huge thanks for your friendship and support of my dreams, and also for your time on our websites. I owe my international online reader-ship to you. Big thanks to the Written Road community for fol-lowing the ride. You make it so much more fun. Love and gratitude to: [Belgium contingent] Jacob, Judy, Simon & Celia, for getting me abroad and all the amazing things that followed; [London contin-gent] Viv, Josh, Peter and Gwyn Spoerri for buying the most copies of *Sand*, and providing the best home office I've ever had; Chris O'Neill, for always having a special occasion to take me to dinner and saying all the right things once we were there; [German con-tingent] The Reiber Family for their warm hospitality and leading me to another adventurous story; [Australian contingent] The Heidrichs and Max & Merle for their continued love and open door policy; [San Diego contingent] Walshs, Buczaczers, and Gimbels for decades of love and support; [Editors-at-Large] Mark Johnson at HotelChatter.com for building my bylines and keeping me on the road, Scott M. Gimple, Jennifer Colvin, Rolf Potts, Jim Benning, Andrew Dean Nystrom, and Barb Shaw—my virtual writers group this time around.

And last but best, my lifelong friends who always get to hear the stories first: Dan Buczaczer, Heather Grennan, Lisa P. Ramsey, Vivienne Spoerri, Bridget Burke Ravissa, the Welshs' and the Lyons.

"The Mile-High and Dry Club" by Cindy Chupack excerpted from *The Between Boyfriends Book* by Cindy Chupack. Copyright © 2003 by Cindy Chupack. Reprinted by permission of St. Martin's Press.

"Blame It on Rio" by Cynthia Barnes published with permission from the author. Copyright © 2004 by Cynthia Barnes.

"Don't Slap the Witchdoctor" by Annie Caulfield excerpted from *Show Me the Magic: Travels Round Benin by Taxi* by Annie Caulfield. Copyright © 2002 by Annie Caulfield. Reprinted by permission of Penguin Books, Ltd.

"When You Gotta Go" by Barbara H. Shaw published with permission from the author. Copyright © 2004 by Barbara H. Shaw.

"Waiting For The Big 'O'" by Felice Prager published with permission from the author. Copyright © 2004 by Felice Prager.

"Emboldened by Women in High Heels" by Anne Calcagno published with permission from the author. Copyright © 2004 by Anne Calcagno.

"Eat My Shorts...If You Can Find Them" by Jenn Dlugos published with permission from the author. Copyright © 2004 by Jenn Dlugos.

"Fruit Bats and Healers" by Ayun Halliday excerpted from *No Touch Monkey! and Other Travel Lessons Learned Too Late* by Ayun Halliday. Copyright © 2003 by Ayun Halliday. Reprinted by permission of Seal Press.

"The Pen is Mightier Than the Prick" by Lara Ephron published with permission from the author. Copyright © 2004 by Lara Ephron.

"Blind Faith" by Susan Lyn McCombs published with permission from the author. Copyright © 2004 by Susan Lyn McCombs.

"The Barf Boat" by Karla Zimmerman published with permission from the author. Copyright © 2004 by Karla Zimmerman.

"The Adventures of MegaChicken" by Rikke Jorgensen published with permission from the author. Copyright © 2004 by Rikke Jorgensen.

"Midmorning Express" by Elizabeth Asdorian published with permission from the author. Copyright © 2004 by Elizabeth Asdorian.

"See How She Runs" by Suzanne Schlosberg published with permission from the author. Copyright © 2004 by Suzanne Schlosberg.

"A Cowboy in Vienna" by Jessica Maxwell published with permission from the author. Copyright © 2004 by Jessica Maxwell.

"Squeaky Clean, and Then Some" by Jennifer L. Leo published with permission from the author. Copyright © 2004 by Jennifer L. Leo.

"Flora and Fauna in Madrid" by Kalpana Mohan published with permis-

Selection from "Kili Me Softly" by Laurie Frankel published with permission from the author. Copyright © 2004 by Laurie Frankel.

Selection from "Looking for Love in All the Wrong Places" by Kathryn Pritchett published with permission from the author. Copyright © 2004 by Kathryn Pritchett.

Selection from "Lost in Las Vegas" by April Thompson published with permission from the author. Copyright © 2004 by April Thompson.

Selection from "Love Potion No.9" by Colleen Friesen published with permission from the author. Copyright © 2004 by Colleen Friesen.

Selection from "Make Mine Me" by Colette O'Connor published with permission from the author. Copyright © 2004 by Colette O'Connor.

Selection from *No Touch Monkey! and Other Travel Lessons Learned Too Late* by Ayun Halliday copyright © 2003 by Ayun Halliday. Reprinted by permission of Seal Press.

Selection from "Saturday Night in the City" by Jennifer Colvin published with permission from the author. Copyright ©2004 by Jennifer Colvin.

Selection from "The Spa Who Loved me" by Suz Redfearn published with permission from the author. Copyright © 2004 by Suz Redfearn.

Selection from *Around the Bloc: My Life in Moscow, Beijing, and Havana* by Stephanie Elizondo Griest copyright © 2004 by Stephanie Elizondo Griest. Used by permission of Villard Books, a division of Random House, Inc.

Selection from "Tick. Tick. Tick." by Kim Steutermann Rogers published with permission from the author. Copyright © 2004 by Kim Steutermann Rogers.

Selection from "Travels with Mom" by Michele Peterson published with permission from the author. Copyright © 2004 by Michele Peterson.

Selection from "The Vacation Purse" by Mona Cleary published with permission from the author. Copyright © 2004 by Mona Cleary.

Selection from "A Whacking in Naples" by Laurel Miller published with permission from the author. Copyright © 2004 by Laurel Miller.

Selection from "'You're Exotic' and Other Cute Things the Locals Said" by Jennifer L. Leo published with permission from the author. Copyright © 2004 by Jennifer L. Leo.

About the Editor

Jennifer L. Leo won an underwear contest her freshman year at USC during a traditional drum line hazing ritual in the Trojan Marching Band. She is the editor of the best-selling *Sand in My Bra and Other Misadventures*, and was awarded a Grand Prize from the North American Travel Journalists Association in 2003. Coeditor of *A Woman's Path*, her writing has also appeared in *A Woman's Passion for Travel, The Adventure of Food*, Lonely Planet World Food Guides *Hong Kong, TIME, STA's Break, Student Traveler*, BootsnAll.com, and HotelChatter.com. Jen is the creator of WrittenRoad, a popular online blog for travel writers. You can follow her adventures at www.JenLeo.com.

TRAVELERS' TALES

THE POWER OF A GOOD STORY

New Releases

THE BEST   **$16.95**
TRAVELERS' TALES 2004
True Stories from Around the World
Edited by James O'Reilly, Larry Habegger & Sean O'Reilly
The launch of a new annual collection presenting fresh, lively storytelling and compelling narrative to make the reader laugh, weep, and buy a plane ticket.

INDIA   **$18.95**
True Stories
Edited by James O'Reilly & Larry Habegger
"*Travelers' Tales India* is ravishing in the texture and variety of tales."
                                    —*Foreign Service Journal*

A WOMAN'S EUROPE   **$17.95**
True Stories
Edited by Marybeth Bond
An exhilarating collection of inspirational, adventurous, and entertaining stories by women exploring the romantic continent of Europe. From the bestselling author Marybeth Bond.

WOMEN IN THE WILD   **$17.95**
True Stories of Adventure and Connection
Edited by Lucy McCauley
"A spiritual, moving, and totally female book to take you around the world and back."   —*Mademoiselle*

CHINA   **$18.95**
True Stories
Edited by James O'Reilly, Larry Habegger & Sean O'Reilly
A must for any traveler to China, for anyone wanting to learn more about the Middle Kingdom, offering a breadth and depth of experience from both new and well-known authors; helps make the China experience unforgettable and transforming.

BRAZIL   **$17.95**
True Stories
Edited by Annette Haddad & Scott Doggett
Introduction by Alex Shoumatoff
"Only the lowest wattage dim bulb would visit Brazil without reading this book."   —Tim Cahill, author of *Pass the Butterworms*

THE PENNY PINCHER'S PASSPORT TO   **$14.95**
LUXURY TRAVEL (2ND EDITION)
The Art of Cultivating Preferred Customer Status
By Joel L. Widzer
Completely updated and revised, this 2nd edition of the popular guide to traveling like the rich and famous without being either describes, both philosophically and in practical terms, how to obtain luxurious travel benefits by building relationships with airlines and other travel companies.

Women's Travel

A WOMAN'S EUROPE $17.95
True Stories
Edited by Marybeth Bond
An exhilarating collection of inspirational, adventurous, and entertaining stories by women exploring the romantic continent of Europe. From the bestselling author Marybeth Bond.

WOMEN IN THE WILD $17.95
True Stories of Adventure and Connection
Edited by Lucy McCauley
"A spiritual, moving, and totally female book to take you around the world and back."
— *Mademoiselle*

A WOMAN'S WORLD $18.95
True Stories of Life on the Road
Edited by Marybeth Bond
Introduction by Dervla Murphy

— ★ ★ ★ —
Lowell Thomas Award
—*Best Travel Book*

A MOTHER'S WORLD $14.95
Journeys of the Heart
Edited by Marybeth Bond & Pamela Michael
"These stories remind us that motherhood is one of the great unifying forces in the world"
— *San Francisco Examiner*

A WOMAN'S PASSION FOR TRAVEL $17.95
More True Stories from A Woman's World
Edited by Marybeth Bond & Pamela Michael
"A diverse and gripping series of stories!"
—Arlene Blum, author of
Annapurna: A Woman's Place

Food

ADVENTURES IN WINE $17.95
True Stories of Vineyards and Vintages around the World
Edited by Thom Elkjer
Humanity, community, and brotherhood comprise the marvelous virtues of the wine world. This collection toasts the warmth and wonders of this large extended family in stories by travelers who are wine novices and experts alike.

FOOD $18.95
A Taste of the Road
Edited by Richard Sterling
Introduction by Margo True

— ★ ★ ★ —
Silver Medal Winner of the Lowell Thomas Award
—*Best Travel Book*

HER FORK IN THE ROAD $16.95
Women Celebrate Food and Travel
Edited by Lisa Bach
A savory sampling of stories by the best writers in and out of the food and travel fields.

THE ADVENTURE OF FOOD $17.95
True Stories of Eating Everything
Edited by Richard Sterling
"Bound to whet appetites for more than food."
— *Publishers Weekly*

THE FEARLESS DINER $7.95
Travel Tips and Wisdom for Eating around the World
By Richard Sterling
Combines practical advice on foodstuffs, habits, and etiquette, with hilarious accounts of others' eating adventures.

Travel Humor

SAND IN MY BRA AND $14.95
OTHER MISADVENTURES
Funny Women Write from the Road
Edited by Jennifer L. Leo
"A collection of ridiculous and sublime travel experiences."
          —San Francisco Chronicle

HYENAS LAUGHED AT ME $14.95
AND NOW I KNOW WHY
The Best of Travel Humor and Misadventure
Edited by Sean O'Reilly, Larry Habegger, and James O'Reilly
Hilarious, outrageous and reluctant voyagers indulge us with the best misadventures around the world.

LAST TROUT IN VENICE $14.95
The Far-Flung Escapades of an Accidental Adventurer
By Doug Lansky
"Traveling with Doug Lansky might result in a considerably shortened life expectancy…but what a way to go."
    —Tony Wheeler, Lonely Planet Publications

NOT SO FUNNY WHEN $12.95
IT HAPPENED
The Best of Travel Humor and Misadventure
Edited by Tim Cahill
Laugh with Bill Bryson, Dave Barry, Anne Lamott, Adair Lara, and many more.

THERE'S NO TOILET PAPER…ON THE ROAD LESS TRAVELED $12.95
The Best of Travel Humor and Misadventure
Edited by Doug Lansky

— ★ ★ ★ —

*Humor Book of the Year
—Independent Publisher's Book Award*

— ★ ★ ★ —

ForeWord Gold Medal Winner— Humor Book of the Year

Travelers' Tales Classics

COAST TO COAST $16.95
A Journey Across 1950s America
By Jan Morris
After reporting on the first Everest ascent in 1953, Morris spent a year journeying across the United States. In brilliant prose, Morris records with exuberance and curiosity a time of innocence in the U.S.

TRADER HORN $16.95
A Young Man's Astounding Adventures in 19th Century Equatorial Africa
By Alfred Aloysius Horn
Here is the stuff of legends—thrills and danger, wild beasts, serpents, and savages. An unforgettable and vivid portrait of a vanished Africa.

THE ROYAL ROAD $14.95
TO ROMANCE
By Richard Halliburton
"Laughing at hardships, dreaming of beauty, ardent for adventure, Halliburton has managed to sing into the pages of this glorious book his own exultant spirit of youth and freedom."
          —Chicago Post

UNBEATEN TRACKS $14.95
IN JAPAN
By Isabella L. Bird
Isabella Bird was one of the most adventurous women travelers of the 19th century with journeys to Tibet, Canada, Korea, Turkey, Hawaii, and Japan. A fascinating read.

THE RIVERS RAN EAST $16.95
By Leonard Clark
Clark is the original Indiana Jones, telling the breathtaking story of his search for the legendary El Dorado gold in the Amazon.

Spiritual Travel

THE SPIRITUAL GIFTS OF TRAVEL $16.95
The Best of Travelers' Tales
Edited by James O'Reilly and Sean O'Reilly
Favorite stories of transformation on the road that shows the myriad ways travel indelibly alters our inner landscapes.

PILGRIMAGE $16.95
Adventures of the Spirit
Edited by Sean O'Reilly & James O'Reilly
Introduction by Phil Cousineau

— ★ ★ ★ —

ForeWord Silver Medal Winner
—Travel Book of the Year

THE ROAD WITHIN $18.95
True Stories of Transformation and the Soul
Edited by Sean O'Reilly, James O'Reilly & Tim O'Reilly

— ★ ★ ★ —

Independent Publisher's Book Award
—Best Travel Book

THE WAY OF THE WANDERER $14.95
Discover Your True Self Through Travel
By David Yeadon
Experience transformation through travel with this delightful, illustrated collection by award-winning author David Yeadon.

A WOMAN'S PATH $16.95
Women's Best Spiritual Travel Writing
Edited by Lucy McCauley, Amy G. Carlson & Jennifer Leo
"A sensitive exploration of women's lives that have been unexpectedly and spiritually touched by travel experiences.… Highly recommended."
    —Library Journal

THE ULTIMATE JOURNEY $17.95
Inspiring Stories of Living and Dying
James O'Reilly, Sean O'Reilly & Richard Sterling
"A glorious collection of writings about the ultimate adventure. A book to keep by one's bedside—and close to one's heart."
    —Philip Zaleski, editor,
    The Best Spiritual Writing series

Special Interest

THE BEST TRAVELERS' TALES 2004 $16.95
True Stories from Around the World
Edited by James O'Reilly, Larry Habegger & Sean O'Reilly
The launch of a new annual collection presenting fresh, lively storytelling and compelling narrative to make the reader laugh, weep, and buy a plane ticket.

TESTOSTERONE PLANET $17.95
True Stories from a Man's World
Edited by Sean O'Reilly, Larry Habegger & James O'Reilly
Thrills and laughter with some of today's best writers: Sebastian Junger, Tim Cahill, Bill Bryson, and Jon Krakauer.

THE GIFT OF TRAVEL $14.95
The Best of Travelers' Tales
Edited by Larry Habegger, James O'Reilly & Sean O'Reilly
"Like gourmet chefs in a French market, the editors of Travelers' Tales pick, sift, and prod their way through the weighty shelves of contemporary travel writing, creaming off the very best."
    —William Dalrymple, author of *City of Djinns*

DANGER! $17.95
True Stories of Trouble and Survival
Edited by James O'Reilly, Larry Habegger & Sean O'Reilly
"Exciting…for those who enjoy living on the edge or prefer to read the survival stories of others, this is a good pick."
    —Library Journal

365 TRAVEL $14.95
A Daily Book of Journeys, Meditations, and Adventures
Edited by Lisa Bach
An illuminating collection of travel wisdom and adventures that reminds us all of the lessons we learn while on the road.

THE GIFT OF RIVERS $14.95
True Stories of Life on the Water
Edited by Pamela Michael
Introduction by Robert Hass
...a soulful compendium of wonderful stories that illuminate, educate, inspire, and delight."
—David Brower, Chairman of Earth Island Institute

FAMILY TRAVEL $17.95
The Farther You Go, the Closer You Get
Edited by Laura Manske
"This is family travel at its finest."
—*Working Mother*

LOVE & ROMANCE $17.95
True Stories of Passion on the Road
Edited by Judith Babcock Wylie
"A wonderful book to read by a crackling fire."
—*Romantic Traveling*

THE GIFT OF BIRDS $17.95
True Encounters with Avian Spirits
Edited by Larry Habegger & Amy G. Carlson
"These are all wonderful, entertaining stories offering a *bird's-eye view!* of our avian friends."
—*Booklist*

A DOG'S WORLD $12.95
True Stories of Man's Best Friend on the Road
Edited by Christine Hunsicker
Introduction by Maria Goodavage

Travel Advice

THE PENNY PINCHER'S PASSPORT TO LUXURY TRAVEL (2ND EDITION) $14.95
The Art of Cultivating Preferred Customer Status
By Joel L. Widzer
Completely updated and revised, this 2nd edition of the popular guide to traveling like the rich and famous without being either describes, both philosophically and in practical terms, how to obtain luxurious travel benefits by building relationships with airlines and other travel companies.

SAFETY AND SECURITY FOR WOMEN WHO TRAVEL $12.95
By Sheila Swan & Peter Laufer
"An engaging book, with plenty of first-person stories about strategies women have used while traveling to feel safe but still find their way into a culture."
—*Chicago Herald*

THE FEARLESS SHOPPER $14.95
How to Get the Best Deals on the Planet
By Kathy Borrus
"Anyone who reads *The Fearless Shopper* will come away a smarter, more responsible shopper and a more curious, culturally attuned traveler."
—Jo Mancuso, *The Shopologist*

SHITTING PRETTY $12.95
How to Stay Clean and Healthy While Traveling
By Dr. Jane Wilson-Howarth
A light-hearted book about a serious subject for millions of travelers— staying healthy on the road—written by international health expert, Dr. Jane Wilson-Howarth.

GUTSY WOMEN $12.95
More Travel Tips and Wisdom for the Road
By Marybeth Bond
Second Edition
Packed with funny, instructive, and inspiring advice for women heading out to see the world.

GUTSY MAMAS $7.95
Travel Tips and Wisdom for Mothers on the Road
By Marybeth Bond
A delightful guide for mothers traveling with their children—or without them!

Destination Titles

ALASKA $18.95
Edited by Bill Sherwonit, Andromeda Romano-Lax, & Ellen Bielawski

AMERICA $19.95
Edited by Fred Setterberg

AMERICAN SOUTHWEST $17.95
Edited by Sean O'Reilly & James O'Reilly

AUSTRALIA $17.95
Edited by Larry Habegger

BRAZIL $17.95
Edited by Annette Haddad & Scott Doggett
Introduction by Alex Shoumatoff

CENTRAL AMERICA $17.95
Edited by Larry Habegger & Natanya Pearlman

CHINA $18.95
Edited by James O'Reilly, Larry Habegger & Sean O'Reilly

CUBA $17.95
Edited by Tom Miller

FRANCE $18.95
Edited by James O'Reilly, Larry Habegger & Sean O'Reilly

GRAND CANYON $17.95
Edited by Sean O'Reilly, James O'Reilly & Larry Habegger

GREECE $18.95
Edited by Larry Habegger, Sean O'Reilly & Brian Alexander

HAWAI'I $17.95
Edited by Rick & Marcie Carroll

HONG KONG $17.95
Edited by James O'Reilly, Larry Habegger & Sean O'Reilly

INDIA $18.95
Edited by James O'Reilly & Larry Habegger

IRELAND $18.95
Edited by James O'Reilly, Larry Habegger & Sean O'Reilly

ITALY $18.95
Edited by Anne Calcagno
Introduction by Jan Morris

JAPAN $17.95
Edited by Donald W. George & Amy G. Carlson

MEXICO $17.95
Edited by James O'Reilly & Larry Habegger

NEPAL $17.95
Edited by Rajendra S. Khadka

PARIS $18.95
Edited by James O'Reilly, Larry Habegger & Sean O'Reilly

PROVENCE $16.95
Edited by James O'Reilly & Tara Austen Weaver

SAN FRANCISCO $18.95
Edited by James O'Reilly, Larry Habegger & Sean O'Reilly

SPAIN $19.95
Edited by Lucy McCauley

THAILAND $18.95
Edited by James O'Reilly & Larry Habegger

TIBET $18.95
Edited by James O'Reilly & Larry Habegger

TURKEY $18.95
Edited by James Villers Jr.

TUSCANY $16.95
Edited by James O'Reilly & Tara Austen Weaver
Introduction by Anne Calcagno

Footsteps Series

THE FIRE NEVER DIES $14.95
**One Man's Raucous Romp Down the Road of Food,
Passion, and Adventure**
By Richard Sterling
"Sterling's writing is like spitfire, foursquare and jazzy with
crackle...."   —*Kirkus Reviews*

ONE YEAR OFF $14.95
**Leaving It All Behind for a Round-the-World Journey
with Our Children**
By David Elliot Cohen
A once-in-a-lifetime adventure generously shared, from the
author/editor of *America 24/7* and *A Day in the Life of Africa*

THE WAY OF THE WANDERER $14.95
Discover Your True Self Through Travel
By David Yeadon
Experience transformation through travel with this delightful,
illustrated collection by award-winning author David Yeadon.

TAKE ME WITH YOU $24.00
A Round-the-World Journey to Invite a Stranger Home
By Brad Newsham
"Newsham is an ideal guide. His journey, at heart, is into
humanity."   —*Pico Iyer, author of* The Global Soul

KITE STRINGS OF THE SOUTHERN CROSS $14.95
A Woman's Travel Odyssey
By Laurie Gough   *ForeWord Silver Medal Winner*
Short-listed for the prestigious Thomas Cook Award, this is an   *— Travel Book of the Year*
exquisite rendering of a young woman's search for meaning.   —— ★ ★ ★ ——

THE SWORD OF HEAVEN $24.00
A Five Continent Odyssey to Save the World
By Mikkel Aaland
"Few books capture the soul of the road like The *Sword of
Heaven,* a sharp-edged, beautifully rendered memoir that will
inspire anyone."
      —Phil Cousineau, author of *The Art of Pilgrimage*

STORM $24.00
**A Motorcycle Journey of Love, Endurance,
and Transformation**   *ForeWord Gold Medal Winner*
By Allen Noren   *— Travel Book of the Year*
"Beautiful, tumultuous, deeply engaging and very satisfying.
Anyone who looks for truth in travel will find it here."   —— ★ ★ ★ ——
      —Ted Simon, author of Jupiter's Travels